Jesus's Truth

Jesus's Truth

Life in Parables

by
Yung Suk Kim

RESOURCE *Publications* • Eugene, Oregon

JESUS'S TRUTH
Life in Parables

Copyright © 2018 Yung Suk Kim. All rights reserved. Except for brief quotations in critical publications or reviews, no part of this book may be reproduced in any manner without prior written permission from the publisher. Write: Permissions, Wipf and Stock Publishers, 199 W. 8th Ave., Suite 3, Eugene, OR 97401.

Resource Publications
An Imprint of Wipf and Stock Publishers
199 W. 8th Ave., Suite 3
Eugene, OR 97401

www.wipfandstock.com

PAPERBACK ISBN: 978-1-5326-4397-2
HARDCOVER ISBN: 978-1-5326-4398-9
EBOOK ISBN: 978-1-5326-4399-6

Manufactured in the U.S.A.

Contents

Acknowledgements | *vii*

Chapter 1
 Introduction | 1
 —Establishing the Original Parables of Jesus

Chapter 2
 Markan Parables | 17
 —Sower
 —Seed Growing Secretly
 —Mustard Seed
 —Tenants
 —Budding Fig Tree

Chapter 3
 Q Parables in Matthew and Luke | 33
 —Leaven
 —Lost Sheep
 —Entrusted Money (Talents)

Chapter 4
 Matthean Unique Parables | 47
 —Wheat and Weed
 —Treasure
 —Pearl
 —Vineyard Workers
 —Unmerciful Servant

—Two Sons
—Great Banquet
—Ten Virgins

Chapter 5
Lukan Unique Parables (I) | 76
—Good Samaritan
—Rich Farmer
—Father and Two Sons

Chapter 6
Lukan Unique Parables (II) | 96
—Unjust Steward
—Rich Man and Lazarus
—Unjust Judge and Widow
—Pharisee and Tax Collector

Bibliography | 111

Acknowledgements

THIS BOOK IS THE result of years of studying and teaching of Jesus's parables. I thank all my students at Samuel DeWitt Proctor School of Theology at Virginia Union University for their diligent study and engagement with my teaching. Through numerous classes taught here, I have become very much motivated to write a new book on the parables of Jesus, which challenge our world today. I also give thanks to the faculty and staff in this great institution. Our new Dean, Dr. Corey Walker, is very supportive my work, and I thank him for his lead and service to our school. I also give special thanks to my colleagues in biblical studies department: Dr. Boykin Sanders and Dr. Robert Wafawanaka. I love their genuine collegial care and support for my life and research. I feel so great and honored to work in this beloved community. I also give my special thanks to Professor Larry Welborn at Fordham University for his sharing of wisdom in New Testament studies and his encouragement to my work. Above all, I cannot forget my wife, Yong-Jeong's sacrifice and love for our family. I also give my special thanks to my daughters (Hyerim, Hyekyung, and Hyein) and my son-in-law (Alex) who are all very supportive of me.

1

Introduction

ALLEGORICAL INTERPRETATION DEPRIVES US of the true meaning of a parable by spiritualizing it. Allegory, derived from *allegorein* (meaning "to speak differently"), is a way of reading the text by focusing not on the internal story but the hidden spiritual meaning. In doing so, what readers do typically is to make a one-to-one correspondence between story and particular outside the story. This allegorical interpretation has been popular with the Alexandrian School (Clement, Origen, and Augustine). In the parable of Samaritan (Luke 10:25-37), the allegorical matchings go like this: Jerusalem as Paradise; Jericho as world; a robbed person as Adam; robbers as evil; priest as the law; Levite as prophets; the good Samaritan as Jesus; injury as disobedience; donkey as Jesus's body; inn as church; the innkeeper as bishop of the church; and the promise of return as the second coming of Jesus. We can hardly think that Jesus applied himself to a Samaritan as in allegorical interpretation. Rather, we can read this parable as a story and wonder why first two religious leaders pass by without helping the needy person. They also have to think about the third person, who is not an ordinary Jewish person but a despised foreigner who need not respond to the needy person from the perspective of Jews. He could pass by without looking at this man robbed, but he stopped by and did everything he could to help him. Hearers must grapple to understand the act of this man from Samaria, a district of contempt by Jews. Who is this guy? He was not considered a neighbor by Jews. But he became a neighbor to them. This mysterious act and presence of the Samaritan raise a metaphorical imagination to hearers.[1] How can a Samaritan become a neighbor? From a traditional perspective of Jews, the neighbor is found among themselves. But the Samaritan became a neighbor to a person in need.

Another famous parable of Jesus, "the father and two sons" (Luke 15:11-34), also has been read allegorically. Namely, the older son/brother represents Jews, the younger son/brother represents newly converted Gentile sinners, and the father represents the compassionate God. So much so, the older brother/son is blamed for his narrow mindset, and his father welcomes the younger brother/son because of his repentance. But inside the parable, there is no such clue that this story is understood with such "representative" interpretation. Rather, this story is taken from everyday life where Jesus emphasizes the importance of mercy and forgiveness in God's rule. Hearers must wonder about the status of a dysfunctional family and the ideal role of each member in eventual reconciliation. Here the metaphorical link is found between God's rule and home.[2] In what way can home be restored to that rule of God so all members are reconciled with each other? What does each person in the family must do toward that goal of peace and reconciliation? This small dysfunctional family is like a broken rule of God in the world.

To avoid allegorical interpretation, we need to put a parable in context. Parables appear both in the Hebrew Bible and the New Testament. The Hebrew *mashal* means "to represent" or "to be like." *Mashals* in the Hebrew Bible include: Jotham's *mashal* of the trees (Judg 9:7-15), Nathan's *mashal* of the poor man's only lamb (2 Sam 12:14), Jehoash's *mashal* of the thistle (2 Kgs 14:9), Isaiah's

---

1. In Amos Wilder's term, the hearer responds to the parable with "emotion, imagination and motivation." Amos Wilder, "Parable of the sower: naivete and method in interpretation," *Semeia*, no 2 1974, p 134-151.

2. Amos Wilder, *The Language of the Gospel: Early Christian Rhetoric* (New York: Harper & Row, 1971), 84.

INTRODUCTION

mashal of the vineyard (Isa 5:16), and Ezekiel's *mashal* of the vine and the eagle (Ezek 17:1-24). In the New Testament, Jesus also tells many parables preserved in the Synoptic Gospels (the Gospel of Thomas, an apocryphal gospel, also contains parables).

The word parable comes from the Greek *parabole*, which means "to be cast alongside."[3] This word has two parts: *para* meaning "alongside" and *bole* meaning "to be cast." So it is "a story cast alongside of life for the sake of leading the audience to see something differently."[4] A parable is a fictional story that employs daily lives and challenges hearers to see beyond their customary views of the world.[5] C. H. Dodd succinctly defines a parable: "At its simplest the parable is a metaphor or simile drawn from nature or common life, arresting the hearer by its vividness or strangeness,

---

3. See David Gowler, *What Are They Saying about the Parables?* (New York, NY: Paulist, 2000), 42-43. See also Claus Westermann, *The Parables of Jesus in the Light of the Old Testament* (Minneapolis, MN: Fortress, 1990), 5-151. See also Brad Young, *The Parables: Jewish Tradition and Christian Interpretation* (Peabody, MA: Hendrickson, 1998), 3-38.

4. Marcus Borg, *Jesus: The Life, Teaching, and Relevance of a Religious Revolutionary* (New York: HaperCollins), 259.

5. Parables belong to a figurative language that is distinguished from plain language. While the former uses a word in a figurative sense, the latter uses it in a plain sense. If we take "water" as an example, "water is clean" is plain language, and "he is like water" is figurative language. Examples of figurative language include metaphor, simile, synecdoche, metonymy, personification, and hyperbole. Metaphor has a structure of "A is B" (for example: "love is war"). A simile has the pattern "A is like B" (example: "Thomas is like a lion"). Synecdoche means that a part of something represents the whole (example: "wheels" for a car). Metonymy means that a thing or concept is called by the name of something else (example: "Hollywood" for the US movie industry). Personification is expressing something with the use of human feeling or action (example: "the wind whispers to me"). Hyperbole uses the language of exaggeration: "I told you a million times." John D. Crossan emphasizes two different functions of figurative language: "One is to illustrate information so that information precedes participation. The other is to create participation so that participation precedes information. The former function produces allegories and examples, pedagogic devices which are intrinsically expendable. The latter produces metaphor on the verbal level and symbol on the nonverbal level." According to him, Jesus's parables should be read as a metaphor that calls for readers' participation. John D. Crossan, *In Parables: The Challenges of the Historical Jesus* (Sonoma, CA: Polebridge, 1992), 14.

3

and leaving the mind in sufficient doubt about its precise application to tease it into active thought."[6] Similarly, Dodd emphasizes both "vividness and strangeness" of a parable through which hearers grapple with an effectively applicable meaning of the parable. All the parables of Jesus are taken from the everyday life: ranging from farming to social life. The parable of the sower is so vivid that hearers can imagine that story as theirs. The parable of the vineyard laborers also reflects the very reality of an economic life in the community. The parable of the leaven is also realistic in ways that people can visualize the process of bread making by a woman. With this vividness of a parable, readers are given the opportunity to rethink what it means to live as God's people or how they can live out the rule of God. The "strangeness" of parable subverts, shatters and reconstructs the hearers' worldview. In the parable of the leaven, there is strangeness because leaven is usually perceived as something corrupt or the seed of evil, as it is associated with a swollen corpse in the street. But Jesus uses it as a metaphor and emphasizes the importance of hidden service or hidden potential in the rule of God. In the parable of the vineyard laborers as well there is strangeness because all workers receive the same amount

6. C. H. Dodd, *The Parables of the Kingdom* (New York: Scribner, 1961), 5. Metaphor links two things together and invites the hearer to ponder on the disparate link between them. A metaphorical statement of "love is war" should be explained by the reader. In what sense is love like war? In what sense is love not like war? Metaphor can be distinguished from simile. While the former invites the hearer to participate in the reality, the latter compares two things. Gowler well summarizes the difference between them: "A simile clarifies the less known by use of the better known in an illustrative fashion: 'A is like B.' ... A metaphor, on the other hand, has a comparison, but it functions in a completely different way because metaphor juxtaposes two discrete and not entirely compatible elements: 'A is B,' so "the metaphor confronts us." See David Gowler, *What Are They Saying about the Parables?* 20. Through this kind of poetic metaphors, Jesus invites hearers to re-imagine the world of God's rule. See J. D. Crossan, *In Parables*, 20. This re-imagined world is not *utopias* that afford consolation but *heterotopias* that are "disturbing, probably because they secretly undermine language." M. Foucault, *The Order of Things* (New York: Pantheon, 1970), xviii. Similarly, Brandon Scott says that "The parables give us access to the way Jesus re-imagined the possibility of living, of being in the world." Bernard Scott, *Re-Imagine the World*, 6.

INTRODUCTION

of a usual daily wage. In this story, Jesus challenges hearers to rethink justice in the community and consider the need for others. He knows how to capture hearers' attention and how to challenge their lives to accept and live with the rule of God in the here and now. His pedagogical style is not didactic but invitational. He does not tell them what to do but invites them to engage with the story. In other words, he never explains the meaning of a parable.[7]

Because of the parable's nature, it has double-entendre. On the one hand, readers may find parables easy to understand because they are taken from everyday life. However, they are very difficult to understand because parables involve figurative language which needs careful attention and skill from the reader. In the parable of the sower (Mark 4:1-20; Matt 13:3-23; Luke 8:5-15; Thom 9), there are at least four metaphors we have to interpret: the sower, soil, the seed, and the harvest. The interpretive task and question are how can we relate God's intent with each of these metaphors? How can we understand a link between God's sovereign rule and metaphorical language? It is like swimming on the surface of a deep sea where we have to decide what to do and how to explore the depths of such a place.

---

7. In the sower's parable, Jesus seems to explain the meaning of the parable. But actually, Mark 4:11-12 is Markan addition and 4:13-20 is his allegorical interpretation. This means only Mark 4:3-8 is the parable proper. In Mark, we know that Jesus teaches the crowds and other people. Unlike Markan comment (4:11-12), Jesus does not speak in parables to block others from knowing the secret of God's rule (*basileia tou theou*). Otherwise, Mark 4:11-12 can be read as Mark's post-event reflection about the reality of non-Christians. Mark 4:12 ("in order that 'they may indeed look, but not perceive, and may indeed listen, but not understand; so that they may not turn again and be forgiven'") is a quote from Isaiah 6:9-10, which is Isaiah's post-theological reflections about why Jerusalem fell and its people suffered. At a surface level, Isaiah seems to say that God is behind the painful fall of Jerusalem as if God planned to destroy it by making his people not be able to perceive the truth. He just reflects on the catastrophe of Judah and its people and relates to God's sovereignty as if destruction happened under God's control. But the fall of Jerusalem happened precisely because the people disobeyed the covenant and suffered the consequences of their disobedience, not God's inability to protect them. Overall, Mark 4:11-12 conveys the difficulty of discipleship and its cost. Some follow Jesus and others do not. Mark explains this consequence by having Jesus speak in parables that are not understandable to the outsiders.

A parable is open-ended, and readers must come up with their responses to it. The case is found in the parable of "the father and two sons" (Luke 15:11-32). The story ends where the father explains to his older brother why he welcomes his younger son. Otherwise, hearers do not know what will happen to this dysfunctional family in the parable. Will this older brother enter his house and talk to his younger brother? Will all of them in the family reconcile with each other eventually? The parable does something to readers/hearers who may re-create their transformative stories through God's presence in the here and now.

Establishing the Original Parables of Jesus

The parable of the lost sheep is found in Matthew and Luke (Matt 18:12-13; Luke 15:46; Thom 107). Though we do not know exactly in which context Jesus spoke this parable, what is obvious is that this parable was edited by both Matthew and Luke in their own ways to fit into their theological agendas. While Matthew interprets the lost sheep as "one of these little ones," Luke reads it in connection with a sinner.[8] In Matthew's vision of God's rule, the least is greater than the prophet (Matt 11:11). Luke, however, uses the same parable of Jesus to support his theology that repentance is more important than anything else. But the parable proper is not about repentance. The parable is a story about the lost sheep, which is found by the shepherd. Indeed, the lost sheep cannot repent either. Nevertheless, Luke reads this parable proper in light of its theology of repentance.

Obviously, we cannot know for sure the original form of Jesus's parable. However, it is not impossible to get close to it if we remove later coloring by the evangelists. The bare fact story goes like this: "Once upon a time, a shepherd had a hundred sheep. Suddenly, he lost one sheep. Then, what would he do? Leaving the ninety-nine, would he not make any and every effort to find it?" In a way, not all shepherds can follow the logic of this story because

---

8. The Gospel of Thomas 107 contains this parable too, in which the lost sheep is understood as the one who is loved.

Introduction

one sheep can be lost and given up in some situations; the culture says the ninety-nine are more important than the one lost. In light of Jesus's storytelling technique characterized by vividness and strangeness, this parable of the lost sheep must be Jesus's. He seems to prefer wholesomeness or completeness even if the ninety-nine might be temporarily jeopardized to achieve that.

If we do not separate the later Matthean addition from the parable of talents in Matt 25:14-30, the message of Jesus would be very confusing or morally dangerous to hearers because the one who is given one talent is harshly punished. So much so, some scholars argue that the master in this parable is evil. He is a tyrant in society who maximizes his profit by harshly managing his slaves.[9] But I do not concur with that reading. In my reading, the master is a good one. The problem is that people read the whole text (Mt 25:14-30) as Jesus's parable. To illustrate, I like to use my experience with one of my friends, who asked me about the perplexity of this parable because of the master's harsh treatment of a slave who is given one talent. He told me that he cannot preach about this parable especially because of the last few verses (vv. 28-30). I told him: "As long as you preach the entire text of the parable without making a distinction between Jesus and Matthew, there is no hope." Actually, verses 28-30 are from Matthew's hands. We know this because, throughout Matthew, one important theme is a final judgment. If we take out these verses, we can see the side of a good master whose major concern is not how much money his slaves made, but how they made use of the talents.

Because Jesus's original parables were orally transmitted and written down by the evangelists sometime after Jesus's death, we can expect there are some differences between Jesus's parables and the ones we have in the Gospels. In order to understand Jesus's story better, we need to assess the earlier forms of his parables. But the difficulty is how we can discern the earlier forms of his

---

9. See Richard Rohrbaugh, "A Peasant Reading of the Talents/Pounds: A Text of Terror?"; William Herzog, *Parables as Subversive Speech: Jesus as Pedagogue of the Oppressed* (Louisville, KY: W/JKP, 1994); Luise Schottroff, *The Parables of Jesus* (Minneapolis: Fortress, 2006).

parables. We can consider the following clues. First, Jesus uses metaphors or simile to give his story to his audience. As a gifted storyteller, Jesus loves to use metaphors taken from nature or the everyday life and to compare God's rule with other things (similes). For example, the parable of the Mustard Seed involves both simile and metaphors: "It is like a mustard seed, which, when sown upon the ground, is the smallest of all the seeds on earth; yet when it is sown it grows up and becomes the greatest of all shrubs, and puts forth large branches, so that the birds of the air can make nests in its shade" (Mk 4:31-32). God's rule is compared to a mustard seed (simile). But this story also involves metaphors: mustard seed, the greatest of all shrubs, large branches, birds, nests, and shade. Certainly, these should not be read as allegory as we pointed out the problematic nature of allegory. Apparently, the form of this parable is a simile, and yet overall, this parable calls for metaphoric re-imagination because God's rule is compared to these metaphors. In other words, hearers have to come up with their responses to the link between God's rule and all these metaphors. Also, Jesus takes the source of this parable from nature such that it seems to be typically his. Though we do not know how close the Markan version of the parable of the mustard seed was to Jesus's original, it seems that Mark inherited and maintained it very well. But one thing is clear from a redaction perspective; that is, the Markan version of this parable was edited by Matthew and Luke. Whereas Mark says the soil sown is *ge* (land), Matthew and Luke say it is *agros* (field) and *kepos* (garden), respectively. The Gospel of Thomas says it is a "cultivated field" (Coptic version). These differences reflect the differences in each community and its theology.

    Second, Jesus's parables, as Dodd suggests, involve the qualities of vividness or strangeness. Parables are not for didactic moral teaching but for "shattering the world" and re-imagining it in a radical light as God's rule in the here and now. We have seen about this in the characteristics of the parables of Jesus. Third, likewise, most of Jesus's parables are open-ended and call for hearers' response. It is the Evangelists who want to close the story and fix its meaning in view of their community context. That is why there are layers of redaction in many parables.

Fourth, Jesus's parables seem to have narrative plot structure. For example, Leaven is a very short parable and yet it has basic plot structure: "The kingdom of heaven is like leaven that a woman took and hid in three measures of flour until all of it was leavened" (Mt 13:33). This parable is a story that involves a character (a woman) who does something with an expected result of it. There is also irony in the parable since God's rule is compared to leaven, which is the symbol of corruption in the culture. Equally ironical is the fact that God's rule is compared to a woman's act of hiding leaven in three measures of flour. Metaphorically, what does leaven represent? What does the woman represent? What is the result of her work? This short parable is full of rich plot structure that involves irony and tension between normative society and the world imagined by this parable.

Fifth, we must place Jesus's parables in his context. In other words, if we find later layers of redaction by the Evangelists, we can remove those and get back to the closer form of his parables. For that purpose, we can think of a few different scenarios concerning parable tradition. First, some parables largely remain unchanged, as we have seen in the parable of the Mustard Seed. Second, other parables do not come from the mouth of Jesus. For example, the parable of fishnet (Mt 13:47-50) reflects the Matthean community's eschatology in that the message is people have to wait until the end without judging each other or others. Similarly, Matthew adds his comments (13:37-43a) to the parable of wheat and tares (13:24b-30) to tell his audience that they have to delay their judgment until last. Third, even the purported parables of Jesus usually go through the heavy hands of the Evangelists who edit them to fit in their theology. A good example of this is found in the parable of tenants (Mk 12:1-8, 9-11; Mt 21:33-39, 40-43; Lk 20:9-15a, 15b-18) in that the Evangelists add their interpretation to emphasize the superiority of the Messiah who seems to build a new Israel.

In order to remove the evangelists' redaction layers to the parables of Jesus, we need to know their community context. Mark emphasizes its distinctive message about Jesus and imminent eschatology. Mark (65-70 CE) addresses a community of people who face persecution and have to decide about their faith in times of trial and difficulty. The way to God is costly, so Jesus as the Son of God must go through the same difficulty because of faith. It is not easy to accept the word of Jesus because it involves a cost. Accordingly, when Mark introduces the parable of the sower (Mark 4:3b-8) to his community, he adds additional elements, one redactional part (vv. 9-13) and one allegorical interpretation (4:14-20). Verses 9-13 reflect the difficulty of understanding Jesus's parables, which then reflects the difficulty of joining the believing community like Mark. Verses 9-13 should be understood in view of consequence or the difficulty of becoming a disciple of Jesus and thus a member of Markan community, because people hear good news but do not understand or follow it. Jesus speaks in parables to let them know of the importance of God's rule, but they are dull in understanding or acting. The result and reason are explained with a consequential theology based on God's providence. Also, the allegorical interpretation of 4:14-20 is a Markan addition and interpretation to the parable proper. This allegorical interpretation emphasizes the importance of good soil which is unlike all other soil conditions where hearers' hearts are not well prepared for the word of God. In an allegory, the sower can be Jesus, the disciples of Jesus, or the leaders of the Markan church, who sow (proclaim) the word (the seed). For various reasons most people do not respond to the word as faithfully as they could because of Satan's work, persecution, and the cares of the world.

But there are also "the ones sown on the good soil: they hear the word and accept it and bear fruit, thirty and sixty and a hundredfold" (4:20). Who are these people? In allegorical interpretation we are not informed of conditions or preparations about good soil. In other words, how can people make or prepare the good soil? This question is actually addressed and answered through the entire Gospel of Mark. Mark 1:1, "The beginning of the good news of Jesus Christ, the Son of God," hints at the theme of good news that has to do with Jesus. The rest of the Gospel talks about the

INTRODUCTION

good news that Jesus proclaims, which is hard to carry out. People and his own disciples seek power and glory rather than a way of life based on service for others (Mark 10:45). The first eight chapters of Mark talk about the power of the good news; yet people and his disciples do not understand what he does because of the cares of the world. To know Jesus's identity is so hard a thing for Jesus's disciples, not to mention for other people. Chapters 9-16 detail a long journey of passion, which further shows the price of love and service, as Jesus says in 10:45: "For the Son of Man came not to be served but to serve, and to give his life a ransom for many." In sum, good conditions for soil have to do with this costly service for others.

Matthew writes his Gospel to the mixed audience of primarily Jewish and secondarily Gentile Christians, and this Gospel (85-90 CE) deals with at least three important issues: 1) how much can Matthew (as a community) keep Jewish tradition or Law?; 2) how much can Matthew open its mission to the Gentile?; 3) how can Matthew maintain its community in tension with the Synagogue? Because of these issues in the community, Matthew is carefully written to address and resolve them. So source parables are filtered through the lens of Matthew and edited to fit in its community context. For example, in the parable of the lost sheep, as we have seen before, Matthew emphasizes the importance of serving "one of the least of these" in the community or society.

Luke writes his Gospel to the predominantly Gentile community so much so that Jesus is claimed as a universal Lord and savior. Luke emphasizes the importance of repentance in the community; therefore, for example, some parables are interpreted for that purpose. In the parable of the lost sheep, a returning sheep is compared to a repentant sinner, which is not part of the original parable. Under the Roman Empire, Luke seems to be very careful about women's role in the church or society. In the parable of the unjust judge, Luke places this woman as a model of persistent prayer, adding his interpretation or comments before and after the parable. But in fact, this parable is not about prayer but about justice seeking. Some feminist scholars point out the Lukan tendency of domesticating women in Luke-Acts.

Parables in The Gospels

Jesus spoke in Aramaic and told parables in the same language. The stories told by Jesus have been circulated and retold and again until they were written down and edited by the Evangelists beginning 70 CE to a late first century. So the parables of Jesus were not only edited but also have been part of a narrative gospel. The Synoptic Gospels include many parables. By source, most parables in Mark became a source for Matthew and Luke independently. Matthew and Luke share parables not found in Mark.[10] There are also unique parables to Matthew (9 total) and Luke (17). Overall, among over 60 parables in the Synoptic Gospels, 27 parables are, more or less, developed parables.[11] See below Tables for detailed lists.

Mark

There are ten parables in Mark and eight are used by Matthew and Luke. Italics show narrative parables. See below the Table 1.

Parable	Mark	Cross reference
Garments & Wineskins	Mk 2:21-22	Mt 9:16-17; Lk 5:36-39; GTh 47b
Strong Man	Mk 3:27	Mt 12:29; Lk 11:21; GTh 35
Sower	Mk 4:3-8	Mt 13:3-9; Lk 8:5-8; GTh 9
Lamp on a Stand	Mk 4:21-25	Mt 5:15; Lk 8:16; 11:33; GTh 33

---

10. Some argue that the Q community and Gospel existed (but was lost) in Galilee after Jesus's death. This community may represent an early form of good news followed by the followers of Jesus, whose teaching is found in the parables found in Matthew and Luke (so Q parables). See John S. Kloppenborg, *Q the Earliest Gospel* (Louisville and London: W/JKP, 2008), 1-97. See also Mark Powelson and Ray Riegert eds. *The Lost Gospel Q: The Original Sayings of Jesus* (Berkeley, CA: Seastone, 1996).

11. Robert Funk, *The Parables of Jesus* (Polebridge Press, 1988), 26-27. Funk lists 33 narrative parables, including non-canonical gospels (6 parables).

INTRODUCTION

Parable	Mark	Cross reference
Seed Growing Secretly	Mk 4:26-29	GTh 21c
Mustard Seed	Mk 4:30-32	Mt 13:31-32; Lk 13:18-19; GTh 20
Salt	Mk 9:50	Mt 5:13; Lk 14:34
Tenants	Mk 12:1-11	Mt 21:33-34; Lk 20:9-18; GTh 65
Budding Fig Tree	Mk 13:28-29	Mt 24:32-33; Lk 21:29-31
Returning Master	Mk 13:33-37	

Matthew

There are 28 parables in Matthew. Italics show narrative parables. Matthew uses 8 of Markan parables. Overall, there are eight parables of the Q and nine unique parables (M). See below the Table 2.

Parable	Matthew	Cross reference
Salt	Mt 5:13	Mk 9:50; Lk 14:34
Lamp on a Stand	Mt 5:15	Mk 4:21; Lk 8:16; 11:33
Going before the Judge	Mt 5:25-26	Lk 12:58-59
Serving Two Masters	Mt 6:24-25	Lk 16:13
Specks and Planks	Mt 7:3-4	Lk 6:41-42
Good and Bad Fruit	Mt 7:16-20	Lk 6:43-44
Two Houses	Mt 7:24-27	Lk 6:47-49
Garment and Wineskins	Mt 9:16-17	Mk 2:21-2; Lk 5:36-39; GTh 47
Children in the Market Place	Mt 11:16-19	Lk 7:31-35
Strong Man	Mt 12:29	Mk 3:27; Lk 11:21; GTh 35
Return of the Unclean Spirit	Mt 12:43-45	Lk 11:24-26
Sower	Mt 13:3-9	Mk 4:3-8; Lk 8:5-8; GTh 9
Wheat and Weed	Mt 13:24-30	GTh 57
Mustard Seed	Mt 13:31-32	Mk 4:30-32; Lk 13:18-19; GTh 20
Leaven	Mt 13:33	Lk 13:20-21; GTh 96
Treasure	Mt 13:44	GTh 109
Pearl	Mt 13:45-46	GTh 76
Net	Mt 13:47-48	GTh 8
Lost Sheep	Mt 18:12-14	Lk 15:3-7; GTh 107
Unmerciful Servant	Mt 18:23-35	
Vineyard Laborers	Mt 20:1-16	
Two Sons	Mt 21:28-32	
Tenants	Mt 21:33-44	Mk 12:1-11; Lk 20:9-18; GTh 65
Great Banquet	Mt 22:1-14	Lk 14:16-24; GTh 64

Parable	Matthew	Cross reference
Budding Fig Tree	Mt 24:32-33	Mk 13:28-29; Lk 21:29-31
Burglar	Mt 24:43-44	Lk 12:39-40; GTh 21b, 103
Entrusted Money	Mt 24:45-51	Lk 12:42-46
Closed Door	Mt 25:1-13	
Entrusted Money	Mt 25:14-30	Lk 19:12-27
Last Judgment	Mt 25:31-46	

Luke

Luke has the most parables among the synoptic. Luke uses 8 of the Markan parables, 13 Q-related parables, and 18 unique parables (L). See below the Table 3.

Parable	Luke	Cross reference
Garment and Wineskins	Lk 5:36-39	Mk 2:21-22; Mt 9:16-17; GTh 47b
Specks and Planks	Lk 6:41-42	Mt 7:3-4
Good and Bad Fruit	Lk 6:43-44	Mt 7:16-20
Two Houses	Lk 6:47-49	Mt 7:24-27
Children in the Market	Lk 7:31-35	Mt 11:16-19
Two Debtors	Lk 7:41-43	
Sower	Lk 8:5-8	Mk 4:3-8; Mt 13:3-9; GTh 9
Lamp on a Stand	Lk 8:16; 11:33	Mk 4:21; Mt 5:15; GTh 33
Samaritan	Lk 10:25-37	
Friend at Midnight	Lk 11:5-8	
Strong Man	Lk 11:21	Mk 3:27; Mt 12:29; GTh 35
Return of the Unclean Spirit	Lk 11:24-26	Mt 12:43-45
Rich Farmer	Lk 12:16-21	GTh 63
Returning Master	Lk 12:35-38	Cf. Mk 13:33-37
Burglar	Lk 12:39-40	Mt 24:43-44; GTh 21b, 103
Servants Entrusted	Lk 12:42-46	Mt 24:45-51
Going before the Judge	Lk 12:58-59	Mt 5:25-26
Barren Fig Tree	Lk 13:6-9	
Mustard Seed	Lk 13:18-19	Mk 4:30-32; Mt 13:31-32; GTh 20
Leaven	Lk 13:20-21	Mt 13:33; GTh 96
Closed Door	Lk 13:24-30	Cf. Mt 25:10-12
Choice of Places at Table	Lk 14:7-11	
Great Banquet	Lk 14:16-24	Mt 22:1-10; GTh 64
Tower Builder	Lk 14:28-30	

INTRODUCTION

Parable	Luke	Cross reference
Warring King	Lk 14:31-33	
Salt	Lk 14:34	Mk 9:50; Mt 5:13
Lost Sheep	Lk 15:3-7	Mt 18:12-13; GTh 107
Lost Coin	Lk 15:8-10	
The Father and Two Sons	Lk 15:11-32	
Unjust Steward	Lk 16:1-8	
Serving Two Masters	Lk 16:13	Mt 6:24-25
Rich Man and Lazarus	Lk 16:19-26	
Servant's Reward	Lk 17:7-10	
Unjust Judge	Lk 18:1-8	
Pharisee and Tax Collector	Lk 18:9-14	
Pounds or Talents	Lk 19:12-27	Mt 25:14-30
Throne Claimant	Lk 19:12, 14-15, 27	
Tenants	Lk 20:9-18	Mk 12:1-11; Mt 21:33-34; GTh 65
Budding Fig Tree	Lk 21:29-31	Mk 13:28-29; Mt 24:32-33

The Gospel of Thomas

There are total 17 parables in the Gospel of Thomas. The idea about the source is hardly recognized in Thomas. Italics show narrative parables. See the Table 4.

Parable	GTh	Cross reference
Net	GTh 8	Mt 13:47-48
Sower	GTh 9	Mk 4:3-8; Mt 13:3-9; Lk 8:5-8
Mustard Seed	GTh 20	Mk 4:30-32; Mt 13:31-2; Lk 13:18-19
Burglar	GTh 21b, 103	Mt 24:43-44; Lk 12:39-40
Seed Growing Secretly	GTh 21c	Mk 4:26-29
Lamp on a tand	GTh 33	Mk 4:21; Mt 5:15; Lk 8:16; 11:33
Strong Man	GTh 35	Mk 3:27; Mt 12:29; Lk 11:21
Garments and Wineskins	GTh 47b	Mk 2:21-22; Mt 9:16-17; Lk 5:36-39
Wheat and Tares	GTh 57	Mt 13:24-30
Rich Farmer	GTh 63	Lk 12:16-21
Great Banquet	GTh 64	Mt 22:1-10; Lk 14:16-24
Wicked Tenants	GTh 65	Mk 12:1-11; Mt 21:33-44; Lk 20:9-18
Pearl	GTh 76	Mt 13:45-46
Leaven	GTh 96	Mt 13:33; Lk 13:20-21
Empty Jar	Gth 97	
Lost Sheep	GTh 107	Mt 18:12-13; Lk 15:3-7
Treasure	GTh 109	Mt 13:44

2

Markan Parables

Sower

MARK 4:3B-8[1]
3 Listen! A sower went out to sow. 4 And as he sowed, some seed fell on the path, and the birds came and ate it up. 5 Other seed fell on rocky ground, where it did not have much soil, and it sprang up quickly, since it had no depth of soil. 6 And when the sun rose, it was scorched; and since it had no root, it withered away. 7 Other seed fell among thorns, and the thorns grew up and choked it, and it yielded no grain. 8 Other seed fell into good soil and brought forth grain, growing up and increasing and yielding thirty and sixty and a hundredfold.

MATTHEW 13:3-9
3 And he told them many things in parables, saying: "Listen! A sower went out to sow. 4 And as he sowed, some seeds fell on the path, and the birds came and ate them up. 5 Other seeds fell on rocky ground, where they did not have much soil, and they sprang up quickly, since they had no depth of soil. 6 But when the sun rose, they were scorched; and since they had no root, they withered away. 7 Other seeds fell among thorns, and the thorns

---

1. All biblical texts are from the NRSV.

grew up and choked them. 8 Other seeds fell on good soil and brought forth grain, some a hundredfold, some sixty, some thirty. 9 Let anyone with ears listen!"

Luke 8:5-8
5 "A sower went out to sow his seed; and as he sowed, some fell on the path and was trampled on, and the birds of the air ate it up. 6 Some fell on the rock; and as it grew up, it withered for lack of moisture. 7 Some fell among thorns, and the thorns grew with it and choked it. 8 Some fell into good soil, and when it grew, it produced a hundredfold." As he said this, he called out, "Let anyone with ears to hear listen!"

Thomas 9
9.1 "Look, a sower went out. He filled his hands (with seeds), (and) he scattered (them). 9.2 Some fell on the path, and the birds came and pecked them up. 9.3 Others fell on the rock, and did not take root in the soil, and they did not put forth ears. 9.4 And others fell among the thorns, they choked the seeds, and worms ate them. 9.5 And others fell on good soil, and it produced good fruit. It yielded sixty per measure and one hundred twenty per measure."

The parable of the sower is the beginning and basis of all other parables.[2] While Klyne Snodgrass calls it "the parable about parables," John Heil says it is "the master parable which holds the key to understanding all the other parables."[3] Indeed, sowing is a most important part of life in an agrarian society. In a way, life begins with sowing without which there will be no harvest. Jesus also

---

2. The parable proper and the evangelist's interpretation should be distinguished. The former includes Mark 4:3b-8, Matt 13:3b-8, Luke 8:5-8a, and the latter Mark 4:14-20, Matt 13:18-23, and Luke 8:11-15. There are also transitional statements between the parable proper and its allegorical interpretation (Mk 4:9-13; Mt 13:9-17; Lk 8:8b-10).

3. Klyne Snodgrass, *Stories with Intent: A Comprehensive Guide to the Parables of Jesus* (Grand Rapids, MI: Eerdmans, 2008), 145. John Heil, "Reader-Response and the Narrative Context of the Parables about Growing Seed in Mark 4:1-34," *Catholic Biblical Quarterly* 54.2 (1992): 278.

begins with this parable when he teaches. Sowing is a human act, but it needs more than that. Ground and seeds are also important. Also, sowing itself is not a goal, and it must be completed with an abundant harvest. The parable of the sower includes at least four distinct metaphors that we have to interpret: the sower, seeds, soil, and the harvest.

The Sower

The sower is the main character in this parable and needs to be carefully observed. He scatters seeds profusely into the ground and gives equal opportunities to the land so it may bear fruit. The sower does not discriminate the land and selects no particular lot to sow. Rather his act of sowing is indiscriminate. He risks some seeds' falling to the unwanted places: the path, on the rock, and among thorns. He has to pay the necessary cost because his goal is to scatter the seeds evenly to all parts of the land. He cannot plant a seed individually. Scattering the seeds, he knows that some will fall outside of the land. But he does not mind losing seeds because they would be nothing as compared to the great harvest.

The sower in this parable does not do a typical way of business in the world, which is based on a cost-benefit analysis. That is, whereas the wise people decide where to invest, the sower in this parable does not decide places to sow the seeds. The sower has reasons for doing this way. First of all, he can maximize the harvest by scattering the seeds. He does not choose the particular ground to sow but uses the wider ground to expect more harvest. This also means that all parts of the land are given the opportunity to receive the seeds. From the seeds' perspective, they are also given more of the opportunity to grow. The sower's profuse scattering of the seeds positively impacts on the destiny of the ground and seed. Second, the sower knows that he will plow the ground after sowing. He is not an idle man who sows and waits until harvest without doing anything. He sows the seeds and later plows the ground. Until the harvest, there are not many things he can do. But plowing is essential.

William Herzog, however, interprets the sower differently, putting him in an unjust, exploitive, economic system.[4] He emphasizes the context of peasant oppression and suffering, based on James Scott's theory of a "hidden transcript," which represents the subordinate group countering a dominant power. The sower is compared to suffering peasants going through turmoil (obstacles of the path, the rocky ground, and thorns that represent the elites' abusive power). The harvest is not his because he is a hired hand.

Seeds

The seeds in this parable are excellent quality. But in reality, there are bad seeds like weeds, as seen in the parable of wheat and weeds. But in this parable, we do not deal with seed quality. The seeds are given to the sower, and they may be the grace of God or the power of life. Once sown on the soil, they must die and then can bear fruit. When the grace of God comes to each person, he/she must die to the self and work for God. This kind of insight about the seed agrees with Jesus's teaching: "Unless a grain of wheat falls into the earth and dies, it remains just a single grain; but if it dies, it bears much fruit" (John 12:24).

Soil

Seeds fall on the four different types of the ground: the path, the rocky ground, the thorns, and the good soil. Jesus does not explain what the four types of the ground mean. While the Evangelists interpret the meaning of the different types of the ground, in his original parable, Jesus does not do so. So essentially, readers have to come up with the conditional realities of the ground in relation to the kingdom of God. One possibility is to think about the person's ability to respond to the word of God. The other possibility is to imagine other realities of life in response to God's rule in the

---

4. William Herzog, "Sowing Discord: The Parable of the Sower (Mark 4:1-9)," *Review and Expositor* 109.2 (2012) 187-198.

world: for example, the personal attitude toward God, the community's culture, and social structure. God's grace or power does not become a reality in a person's life or in the world if all these realities resist taking roots. Among the four types, good soil is the only one that bears fruit. But what is good soil? The parable does not tell us about it. Good soil is not a given but is made by the sower who will plow after sowing. Good soil must look like the weed-free ground with soft earth. The weed-free ground may be a person's pure heart toward God and others. It may also mean the community's genuine love and spirit toward all of its members. The soft earth may be a mind of mercy and compassion shown in persons or in the community that sees the need of the marginalized first. Good soil is that which accepts all kinds of seeds and grows them. As the sower is impartial, so the good soil is.

Harvest

In the end, the sower's best moment of life comes with a great harvest. This is a time of celebration that families come together to remember harsh times of sowing and plowing and to thank God for the weather and rain permitting for the harvest. The best thing comes at last, not in the beginning or in the middle. So waiting is also important after sowing and plowing are done. In agriculture, a harvest is the end product, but life does not end with that. There will be again the next round of work in the next season: sowing, plowing, and waiting for the harvest. Life moves on with this cyclical rhythm of life in which both humans and God work together.

Questions for Reflection/Discussion

1. What would be the best title for this parable?
2. This parable does not explain about good soil. What makes up the good soil?

3. Where else in the Gospels does Jesus teach the importance of God's impartial love?

Seed Growing Secretly

> MARK 4:26-29
> 26 He also said, "The kingdom of God is as if someone would scatter seed on the ground, 27 and would sleep and rise night and day, and the seed would sprout and grow, he does not know how. 28 The earth produces of itself, first the stalk, then the head, then the full grain in the head. 29 But when the grain is ripe, at once he goes in with his sickle, because the harvest has come."

The parable of the seed growing secretly, preserved only in Mark, follows the parable of the sower in Mark 4. While the parable of the sower focuses on the sower's action of scattering of seed, this parable highlights growing, and there is no big role of the sower other than planting the first time.[5] In the parable of the sower (Mk 4:1-20), the sower has a greater responsibility about the laborious scattering of seeds and where to sow them without giving up. But in this parable, the role of the sower is very different and limited. After sowing, he goes home to sleep and does nothing other than watching seed's growing. The sower even does not know how the seed grows. The sower hardly can be imagined as a God because of this. This underlines the importance of patience and God's timing.[6]

This must be a shock to Jesus's audience as they think they handle everything from sowing to harvest. That is a great misunderstanding.[7] They cannot make seeds and grow them. The seed

---

5. John Heil, "Reader-Response and the Narrative Context of the Parable about Growing Seed in Mark 4:1-34," *CBQ* 54 (1992) 282-83; Eugene LaVerdiere, "Teaching in Parables," *Emmanuel* 94 (1988) 453.

6. Barbara Reid, *Parables of Preachers*, Year B (Collegeville, MN: Liturgical Press, 1999), 66. For example, some Jewish sects such as the armed resistance group (Fourth Philosophy) or some Pharisees were impatient with the slow coming of God's Kingdom.

7. A similar motif is found in 1 Cor 3:6-7 when Paul says like this: "I

has life within it. Once sown to the ground, the sun and good weather help them to grow. The good soil accepts the scattered seeds and provides them necessary ingredients so they may grow. Once the seed is sown, he has to wait until the harvest. There is a process of growing until the harvest: first the stalk, then the head, then the full grain in the head. There is order in growing. Likewise, God's rule can be realized gradually, small by small.

There will be a time of harvest. If there is a beginning, there will also be an end. The sower should wait patiently for this time, hoping to gather the ripened grain. The sower should know a time of the harvest and takes a one-time radical action for it. This means that if one is nurtured enough in the community, he/she must act rapidly for the rule of God. There is a time to grow, and there is a time to serve. One cannot make God's rule happen. A person's job is to realize various gifts of God in the world and share them with others. There must be God's time or job that cannot be overwritten by any person or organization.[8] God is the owner of life and the world, and humans participate in that world with patience.

Questions for Reflection/Discussion

1. List things that only God can do. What are things we must do?
2. In the rule of God, why is the process or order important?
3. Compare the image of the sower in this parable with that of the parable of the sower. What are similarities and differences?

---

planted, Apollos watered, but God gave the growth. So neither the one who plants nor the one who waters is anything, but only God who gives the growth."

8. Raymond Collins, "The Story of a Seed Growing by Itself. A Parable for Our Times," *Emmanuel* 94 (1988) 446-52; Joachim Jeremias, *The Parables of Jesus* (New York: Scribner's Sons, 1972), 151-3.

Mustard Seed

MARK 4:30-32
30. He also said, "With what can we compare the kingdom of God, or what parable will we use for it? 31. It is like a mustard seed, which, when sown upon the ground, is the smallest of all the seeds on earth; 32. yet when it is sown it grows up and becomes the greatest of all shrubs, and puts forth large branches, so that the birds of the air can make nests in its shade."

MATT 13:31-32
31. He put before them another parable:"The kingdom of heaven is like a mustard seed that someone took and sowed in his field; 32. it is the smallest of all the seeds, but when it has grown it is the greatest of shrubs and becomes a tree, so that the birds of the air come and make nests in its branches."

LUKE 13:18-19
18. He said therefore, "What is the kingdom of God like? And to what should I compare it? 19. It is like a mustard seed that someone took and sowed in the garden; it grew and became a tree, and the birds of the air made nests in its branches."

THOM 20
20 The disciples said to Jesus: "Tell us whom the kingdom of heaven is like!" He said to them: "It is like a mustard seed. <It> is the smallest of all seeds. But when it falls on cultivated soil, it produces a large branch (and) becomes shelter for birds of the sky."

The Mustard Seed is found in the Synoptic Gospels and the Gospel of Thomas. It is likely from Jesus because it is attested in multiple independent sources. More than that, Jesus's use of the mustard seed as a figure for God's rule seems strange and surprising because the right metaphor for God's rule in Jewish tradition is a cedar tree (Ezek 17:22-23). While the cedar is the symbol of Israel or greatness, the mustard seed is that of smallness.[9] The mustard seed represents the smallest seed. Now with this parable, Jesus zeroes in on another aspect of God's rule that stresses the importance of smallness in God's rule. The challenge of this parable is given to the culture of Jesus's time that seeks greatness like a cedar tree. The mustard seed or plant does not appear in Jewish tradition or scriptures. Even though the mustard seed does not grow into a big tree like a cedar tree, its growth to several feet high is a miracle.

Interestingly, while the mustard seed is planted on the ground (*ge*) in Mark, other Gospels place the seed in different soil conditions: field (*argos*) in Matthew, garden (*kepos*) in Luke, and "tilled ground" in the Gospel of Thomas. It is believed that Mark preserves or inherits a good reliable oral tradition from Jesus because Jesus's proclamation of God's rule is focused on God's impartial love. Ground (*ge*) in Mark means a universal place that God's rule must be implanted. In contrast, Matthew, Luke, and Thomas change "ground" to field, garden, and tilled ground, respectively, to fit in their community context or theology. In Matthew, "field" represents his community that must be cultivated. In Luke, "garden" represents his urban-centered Gentile community, one of Lukan emphases in his gospel. In Thomas, "tilled ground" means the intellectual readiness for the rule of God. Because of the Gnostic idea that knowledge is more important than faith, Thomas underscores "preparation" of the ground.

Mark says it is "the smallest of all the seeds on earth" while Matthew says it is "the smallest of all the seeds." However, Luke deletes the description about the size of the seed. In reality, the mustard seed is not the smallest seed on earth or the smallest seed of all the seeds. There is an 85 micrometers seed in the world which is invisible to human eyes. However, Mark or Matthew's description may not be false if the village tradition in Galilee believes the mustard seed is the smallest of all the seeds in their knowledge or tradition. So there is nothing wrong with the evangelists' description.

---

9. For discussion about the role of cultural repertoire in this parable, see Ryan S. Schellenberg, "Kingdom as Contaminant? The Role of Repertoire in the Parables of the Mustard Seed and the Leaven," *CBQ* 71.3 (2009) 527-543.

Jesus's Truth

It is metonymy, which is a figure for name change; Hollywood for movie industry or Wall Street for the financial industry. A mustard seed simply means a small seed. Luke deleted the description about the size of the seed because the mustard seed is not the smallest or because there is no need to explain about the size of the seed since it is well known to his audience. The important thing is not about whether this seed is the smallest on earth or among all the seeds. The parable is not about horticulture or science.

Three evangelists do not exactly agree on details about the growth of the mustard seed. According to Mark, it "becomes the greatest of all shrubs, and puts forth large branches, so that the birds of the air can make nests in its shade" (Mk 4:32). In Matthew, "it is the greatest of shrubs and becomes a tree, so that the birds of the air come and make nests in its branches" (Mt 13:32). Now Luke says: "It grew and became a tree, and the birds of the air made nests in its branches" (Lk 13:19). Mark's description is realistic as we observe the mustard seed does not grow into a real tree from the normative perspective of society. From a perspective of arboreal science, the mustard plant is not a tree. But from the perspective of evangelists, it is a tree. Why not? According to Mark, it puts forth large branches so the birds of the air can make nests in its shade. The branches of the mustard plants are strong enough, and its shade is good enough for the birds of the air. So Matthew and Luke are right in saying the mustard seed becomes a tree. That is a tree. The mustard plant is strong enough and serves the birds of the air and people who need it for food or medicine. The mustard plant is a beautiful tree on its own, though unlike the tallest tree in the world.

But, the mustard plant or tree is incomparable with a cedar tree, the king of the trees, growing on the high snowy mountains in Lebanon, 2000m from the sea level; its height is 40m high; its diameter of 3m, and lifespan of 2-3000 years. The cedar tree appears 70 times in the OT; it is the deluxe wood material used for palaces (Ps 104:16). Cedar represents glory (Isa 35:2, 60:13), power (Ps 29:5), magnificence (1 Kgs 19:23; Isa 2:13), and authority (1 Kgs 4:33, 2 Kgs 14:9, Zech 11:1). But Jesus surprises his audience by telling them that God's kingdom is like a mustard seed. The following is an imaginable parody given by Jesus:

> You may think of the mustard seed too small that nothing would be possible. But it is a tree and on it, the birds of the air can make nests; you are not the only tree or branches the birds visit. Don't boast about your size. If you are arrogant, who can make nests on you? You are not the only tree. There are many trees and plants in the world. The mustard plant is also a tree that birds come and make nests.

The mustard seed grows to several meters only, living only a few years. It can be found easily nearby the village. It is strong to diseases and spread wildly. The image of abundance fills the whole mountain or field. Not an individual beauty but a collective beauty. See how useful the mustard plant is for everyday people in Galilee. Though the mustard tree or plant grows about several feet high, living only a few years, it grows big enough to serve the birds of the air and make people happy by providing them with food or medicine. It is found everywhere and spread like wildfire and covers the whole mountain and fields nearby their home. They are so beautiful not because of their size but because of their use and collective beauty where all grow together to serve the birds and people. Do you like one tall lonely tree like a cedar tree or do you want to grow together for the community? Also, birds make nests on the branches of the mustard plant. A new life begins here with the small tree.

During Jesus's time success is measured by wealth and status. According to this worldview, the mustard seed/plant is a failure—incomparable with the beautiful cedar trees. Even though the mustard plant is not among the tallest trees like the cedar, it grows hundreds of times from a small seed. That is a miracle. It is a big success. The mustard plant must be measured by its own.[10] Like the mustard plant, each person or the community has the potential that should be realized. Otherwise, this parable is not about

---

10. Harvey McArthur, "The Parable of the Mustard Seed," *CBQ* 33.2 (1971) 198-210.

growth alone but about smallness, which is an important virtue in the kingdom of God. No plant grows in one day. A thousand-mile trip must begin from under one's feet. No success would be possible if small is ignored.

Questions for Reflection/Discussion

1. Is a mustard plant a tree? Can this parable be read as a parody that pokes at the cedar tree?
2. How does smallness in the rule of God apply to us?
3. Read Mark 10:41-45 and find smallness that Jesus refers to.

Tenants

MARK 12:1-12 (CF. MATT 21:33-46; LUKE 20:9-18; GOS. THOM. 65-66)

1 Then He began to speak to them in parables: "A man planted a vineyard and set a hedge around *it*, dug a place for the wine vat and built a tower. And he leased it to vinedressers and went into a far country. 2 "Now at vintage-time he sent a servant to the vinedressers, that he might receive some of the fruit of the vineyard from the vinedressers. 3 "And they took him and beat him and sent him away empty-handed. 4 "Again he sent them another servant, and at him they threw stones, wounded him in the head, and sent him away shamefully treated. 5 "And again he sent another, and him they killed; and many others, beating some and killing some. 6 "Therefore still having one son, his beloved, he also sent him to them last, saying, 'They will respect my son.' 7 "But those vinedressers said among themselves, 'This is the heir. Come, let us kill him, and the inheritance will be ours.' 8 "So they took him and killed him and cast him out of the vineyard. 9 "Therefore what will the owner of the vineyard do? He will come and destroy the vinedressers, and give the vineyard to others. 10 "Have you not even read

this Scripture: 'The stone which the builders rejected Has become the chief cornerstone. 11 This was the LORD's doing, And it is marvelous in our eyes'?" 12 And they sought to lay hands on Him, but feared the multitude, for they knew He had spoken the parable against them. So they left Him and went away.

This parable differs from the irenic "seed" parables and deals with social issues entangled with slave-master relationships. In the first century CE, many peasants lost their lands because of heavy taxes or famine. So we can think of this parable as reflecting uneasy relationships between peasants and landlords in first-century Palestine. There were peasant uprisings in Galilee before and after Jesus's time.[11]

This parable is one of the difficult parables to understand because it is ambiguous (verse 8 or 9a).[12] Besides, it is hard to know in what context Jesus told this parable (verses 1-9). More difficulty lies in Mark's allegorical interpretation in verses 10-12. This parable echoes servant stories in the Hebrew Bible (Jer 7:25; 25:4; Amos 3:7; Zech 1:6). Especially, it has an immediate echo in Isaiah 5:1-7 where God plants choice vines in his vineyard. But it produces wild grapes; so God judges his vineyard, which means his people. But in this parable, the master judges not the vineyard but the tenants.

There are three choices of interpretation for this parable. First, we can read this parable as Jesus's own which ends either at verse 8 or 9a. If it ends at verse 8 ("So they took him and killed him and cast him out of the vineyard"), the implied meaning is that peasants should be united to resist the harsh rule. So the parable favors a violent resistance to realize justice to them. But if the parable ends at v.9a ("Therefore what will the owner of the vineyard do?"), the implied meaning is to stress non-violent resistance.

11. Douglas Oakman, *Jesus and the Economic Questions of His Day* (Edwin Mellen, 1987), 57-72.
12. For a review of recent scholarship on this parable, see Klyne Snodgrass, "Recent Research on the Parable of the Wicked Tenants: An Assessment," *Bulletin of Biblical Research* 8 (1998) 187-216.

Second, we can read this parable (verses 1-12) from Mark's perspective. Mark reads the parable allegorically and adds more to Jesus's original parable, applying the owner of the vineyard to God, vineyard to Israel, servants to the prophets, the beloved son to Jesus, tenants to Jewish leaders, and those who inherit the vineyard to Gentile Christians. So Mark's interpretation is done through Christological concerns that Jesus is the Messiah.

Third, since we do not know the exact setting of this parable or how much the original parable of Jesus was modified by the early Church, we must raise questions such as: How can we interpret the master's harsh judgment? How can we evaluate the peasants' loss of the land? What can we say about violent resistance? Eventually, it is readers' job to answer or to take a stand.

Mark reads this parable allegorically by adding more details as we saw before. But there are positive things about the Markan community's eschatology and its ethics. If this parable is seen from a perspective of a godly vineyard, it shows the importance of the universal kingdom of God. God is the owner of the vineyard (the world), and all people are tenants. But the world in the eyes of Mark faces many evil and injustices. That means that God's vineyard was not taken care of due to many thieves and evil people. So to the community of Mark, Jesus is the Son of God who cares for the kingdom of God. Like Jesus, the community must follow the way of his faith and his sacrifice for the kingdom of God. All people in the world are tenants and therefore must serve others as Jesus did. That is the Markan community's kingdom principle.

Questions for Reflection/Discussion

1. Why were so many tenants in the first century and how can you describe this situation?

2. To what does the vineyard refer? Is it Israel, church, or the world?

3. If we are all tenants in God's vineyard, what is the desirable work ethic? (Read Ps 91:1-16; 112:1-6).

MARKAN PARABLES

Budding Fig Tree

MARK 13:28-32 (CF. MATT 24:32-36; LUKE 21:29-33)
18 "From the fig tree learn its lesson: as soon as its branch becomes tender and puts forth its leaves, you know that summer is near. 29 So also, when you see these things taking place, you know that he is near, at the very gates. 30 Truly I tell you, this generation will not pass away until all these things have taken place. 31 Heaven and earth will pass away, but my words will not pass away. 32 "But about that day or hour no one knows, neither the angels in heaven, nor the Son, but only the Father.

This parable deals with eschatology—things about the end. When things go rough, humans, ancient or today, yearn for a new world. Apocalyptic literature plays a role of comforting the troubled hearts in a time of crisis. Jews produced lots of apocalyptic literature between 200 BCE and 200 CE to deal with the problem of evil and suffering of the innocent. The typical apocalyptic message is that God will prevail and until then people must stay in the faith. So many people in the first century thought apocalyptically.[13]

With this above in mind, it is easy to read this parable from the apocalyptic perspective. So the whole parable draws from Jesus, who asks people to be awake and to do God's work. Because no one knows for sure when such an end comes, he/she should be awake. So it may be the case that Jesus said verse 30 ("this generation will not pass away until all these things have taken place"). If Jesus said this, he must have been an apocalyptic prophet, who predicted the imminent end of the world. But scholars remain divided over whether he was an apocalyptic prophet or a social reformer/sage who taught about the coming of God's rule (cf. Mark 1:14-15; Luke 17:21; John 14:6). But given Mark 9:1 and the overall community situation in Mark, the imminence of the end seems to come from Mark, who believes the end is soon to come. Like a budding fig tree, the community must believe that they will be

---

13. Barbara Reid, *Parables for Preachers*, Year B, 84.

hopeful because God will bring a victory to the world. Here the use of a budding fig tree symbolizes a new life in Christ.[14]

This parable of the Budding Fig Tree fits well in Mark that awaits the coming of the Lord. While the world at large is tough for the Markan community because of political and social pressures, they have to stick to their faith that Jesus is the Messiah, who leads people into the kingdom of God. They believe that God will take upside down the current system and complete the kingdom of God. Therefore, until then, the community must persevere in faith and hope for the day of the eventual salvation. In this respect, this parable works as an apocalyptic literature that helps to assure the Markan community with an eventual victory of God.

Questions for Reflection/Discussion

1. What is your view of eschatology?
2. Think about the role of apocalyptic literature. In times of suffering or hardships, how is theodicy (justice of God) talked and resolved? Read also Psalm 13 or Job.
3. What must be the right attitude toward the end?

---

14. Ibid., 87.

3

Q Parables in Matthew and Luke

Leaven

MATT 13:33
He told them another parable: "The kingdom of heaven is like leaven that a woman took and mixed in with three measures of flour until all of it was leavened."

LUKE 13:20-21
And again he said, "To what should I compare the kingdom of God?21 It is like leaven that a woman took and mixed in with three measures of flour until all of it was leavened."

THOMAS 96
Jesus [said], The Father's kingdom is like [a] woman. She took a little leaven, [hid] it in dough, and made it into large loaves of bread. Anyone here with two ears had better listen!

WHILE MATTHEW AND LUKE share the same version of the story, Thomas's version is disparate since it directly links the kingdom of God with a woman, which is believed to be a later tradition.[1]

1. Whereas both Matthew and Luke compare the kingdom with leaven, Thomas links it to a woman. Against the majority of scholars who believe that

Jesus's Truth

This parable must be one of the most genuine parables of Jesus since it is untraditional and challenging. Leaven is hardly used as a metaphor for positive meanings. Rather, it represents someone or something that is corruptible or evil. Leaven in literature and culture in this time is used so negatively so that no one can imagine using it positively. Leaven is a symbol of corruption or rotten image like a corpse on the streets. In other places in the New Testament, even Jesus and Paul use leaven as a negative metaphor, referring to the source of evil. Jesus warns about the Pharisees' leaven (Mk 8:15; Mt 16:6; Lk 12:1). Similarly, Paul does so (1 Cor 5:6-8; Gal 5:9). But Jesus breaks down such a negative use of it. He imagines of the positive role of leaven in bread making. Is it possible to use leaven in such positive way? The answer is a resounding yes. Leaven has a positive role in bread making. We must look at a word in context. Therefore, leaven in bread making is good, positive, and important. In that, there is nothing wrong with it. Nobody will put leaven to corrupt the bread. Leaven helps to make bread tasty. It also softens flour and spreads good decay to all flour. People can eat delicious bread with joy and thanksgiving.

Even in the Hebrew Bible and Jewish tradition, leaven is not considered corrupt because it is leaven. At Passover, people must clean it from all houses not because it is impure but because they have to keep the day holy and special, remembering God's deliverance that took place in such a short time. At Passover, they do not have time to bake bread with leaven and so have to bake bread without it (Exod 12:17-20). It is a special time of remembering and eating the bread with tears. Such unleavened bread becomes a symbol of difficulties and joyful thanksgiving because of God's grace. But God's people do not eat unleavened bread every day or throughout the year. On pleasant days they eat leavened bread. In the Temple, they eat such delicious bread together (Lev 7:13; 23:17; Amos 4:5). They also eat it on the festival of Weeks. Jewish

---

the referent of leaven may be an earlier tradition about Jesus's parable, Elizabeth Waller argues that the referent of woman is earlier. See Elizabeth Waller, "The parable of the leaven: a sectarian teaching and the inclusion of women," *Union Seminary Quarterly Review* 35.1-2 (1979-80) 99-109.

literature before Jesus (ex: Philo) also deals with the good role of leaven: perfect bread, joy springing from it.

The parable of the leaven is found in Matthew, Luke, and Gospel of Thomas. In Matthew, this parable follows the earlier three parables about the seed and harvest (the Sower, Wheat and Weeds, and Mustard Seed). This order of the parables makes sense to a farming community: from field work to bread making. Using the grain of harvest from the field, women make bread at home. This parable is a story of joy and thanksgiving in the family or community. "Three measures of flour" symbolizes such events of hospitality as shown with Sarah and Hannah in the Hebrew Bible (Gen 18:6; 1 Sam 1:24).

God's rule is compared to a woman who took and hid leaven in the three measures of flour until all are leavened. We have to see what leaven does in bread making. We also have to see what the woman is doing here and how her work relates to God's rule. We also have to see the result of bread making: feast and joy. As we will see, the most important verb in the woman's act is "to hide" (*encrypto*).[2] We have to see both the work of leaven and that of the woman. Leaven's smallness implies the existence of the weak or the vulnerable in society.[3] The small leaven has great potential, but if it remains in its place, it is useless. When taken by the woman and used in the right place, it does great work. Flour cannot change itself without leaven. And leaven cannot change others without the woman who put it in the right place. Her purpose must be to serve the family or guests at dinner. "Three measures of flour" reminds us of Sarah's preparing of bread for the visiting guests (Gen 18:6; cf. Judg 6:19).[4] Like leaven, God's people must work for God and the world without boasting.

---

2. For example, see Robert W. Funk, "Beyond Criticism in Quest of Literacy: the Parable of the Leaven," *Interpretation* 25.2 (1971) 149-170.

3. Bernard B. Scott, *Re-Imagine the World*, 21-34.

4. J. Jeremias, *Parables of Jesus*, 147.

Jesus's Truth

Questions for Reflection/Discussion

1. Does Jesus positively use leaven about God's rule?
2. What are most important roles of leaven in bread making? Relate them to the rule of God.
3. What are important works done by the woman? Relate them to the rule of God.
4. What other parables of Jesus have similar themes of smallness or hiddenness in the rule of God?

Lost Sheep

MATT 18:12-14
12 What do you think? If a shepherd has a hundred sheep, and one of them has gone astray, does he not leave the ninety-nine on the mountains and go in search of the one that went astray? 13 And if he finds it, truly I tell you, he rejoices over it more than over the ninety-nine that never went astray. *14 So it is not the will of your Father in heaven that one of these little ones should be lost.*

LUKE 15:3-7
3 So he told them this parable: 4 "Which one of you, having a hundred sheep and losing one of them, does not leave the ninety-nine in the wilderness and go after the one that is lost until he finds it? 5 When he has found it, he lays it on his shoulders and rejoices. 6 And when he comes home, he calls together his friends and neighbors, saying to them, 'Rejoice with me, for I have found my sheep that was lost.' *7 Just so, I tell you, there will be more joy in heaven over one sinner who repents than over ninety-nine righteous persons who need no repentance.*

GOS. THOM 107
Jesus said, The kingdom is like a shepherd who had a hundred sheep. One of them, the largest, went astray.

He left the ninety- nine and looked for the one until he found it. After he had toiled, he said to the sheep, 'I love you more than the ninety- nine.'

The parable of the lost sheep appears in Matthew, Luke, and Thomas. The source of this parable is a hypothetical source called Q. But both Matthew and Luke significantly edited the source parable to fit into their theological agenda. While Matthew emphasizes the importance of "one of these little ones" which is the wandering sheep, Luke underscores the importance of the lost (sinners or tax-collectors) who repent and return to God.[5] Because of this heavy redaction or allegorizing, some suggest the Thomas version is earlier and takes a more primitive theology of Jesus.[6] One of the main reasons for this view is that "the largest" sheep lost in Thomas is compared to Israel, as Jesus in Matthew says his mission is for the lost sheep of Israel. Even in the Old Testament one of the frequent metaphors is that God seeks and saves the lost one, Israel (Jer 27:17; Isa 53:6). But while this idea the lost sheep refers to Israel is interesting, Gnostic Christians argue that they are the largest. This version in Thomas is more likely a reflection of much later Gnostic tradition.[7] Similarly, in this version, there are Gnostic themes of love and priority for the largest: "One of them, the largest, went astray. He left the ninety- nine and looked for the one until he found it. After he had toiled, he said to the sheep, 'I love you more than the ninety- nine."

If we eliminate the evangelists' redaction part, Jesus's parable must be simple. A shepherd had a hundred sheep and lost one. Then leaving the ninety-nine, will he not go out to search for one lost, wandering sheep? If a sheep is found, how much he will rejoice? This simple yet challenging story is told and retold after

---

5. In fact, the idea that the lost sheep repents is weird because it cannot repent. The point of the parable is not really about the lost sheep which repented and returned but about the good shepherd who sought it with all cost. Amy-Jill Levine, *Short Stories by Jesus*, 27.

6. William L. Petersen, "The Parable of the Lost Sheep in the Gospel of Thomas and the Synoptics," *Novum Testamentan* 23.2 (1981) 44-57.

7. For example, see Robert Grant and D. Freedman, *The Secret Sayings of Jesus according to the Gospel of Thomas* (London, 1960), 181.

Jesus, and the evangelists also told this parable in their own ways. But we are interested in the story of Jesus, who wants to challenge his audience about true leadership. He describes those who are lost as "sheep without a shepherd" (Mt 9:36; cf. 10:6; 15:24). Number one signifies the negligible element in the community. While sinners, tax collectors, the poor, the marginalized, and foreigners are non-existent, leaders of society, political or religious, seek their own power and wealth. So Jesus tells a parable about this situation and challenges the leaders to take care of all sheep.

Good Shepherd

The good shepherd will not leave the ninety-nine abandoned when he goes out to search for the one lost. While some interpret the shepherd risks the safety of the ninety-nine sheep,[8] that seems off the point of this parable, as Osterley notes: "an Oriental parabolist keeps the central point in his teaching in the forefront . . . The central point here is the seeking of the lost sheep, the rest of the flock are not just now in question."[9] If the shepherd could leave the ninety-nine unattended in search of just one lost sheep, he must be absurd. No one can justify that the ninety-nine could be sacrificed for just one. So the possible scenario is that he would ask one of his companions to take care of them while he is in search of the lost one.[10] The good shepherd will not give up the one lost because it is so valuable to him, and all sheep are equally important and valuable. The good shepherd also knows the time that he lost a sheep. The parable suggests the shepherd immediately detects the loss of one sheep—one out of a hundred sheep. The shepherd's timely awareness is possible because he keeps watching all sheep. He has a love for all. Otherwise, he could have gone too far without even knowing about the loss. Late awareness of the loss will not save the

---

8. Findlay, *Jesus and His Parables*, 35.

9. W.O.E Oesterley, *The Gospel Parables*, 176-181.

10. A similar idea like mine is found with Eric F. Fox, "The Parable of the Lost or Wandering Sheep: Matthew 18:10-14; Luke 15:3-7," *Anglican Theological Review* 44.1(1962): 50 (44-57).

lost one because it may be hurt or even be eaten by the wolf. It is also possible the bad shepherd will not notice the loss until he gets home. But essentially, timely awareness alone cannot save the lost one. The good shepherd takes an immediate action to find the lost one. He does everything he could to find it. One sheep is so dear to him. It is part of his life. If he loses one sheep, it is like losing all.

In conclusion, one out of a hundred sheep may be insignificant to the bad shepherd, but the good shepherd cares for every sheep in his hand. In the Hebrew Bible, God is compared to a shepherd and his people are sheep (Ps 23). Jewish leaders are also referred to as shepherds who have to lead the people and take care of them (Ezek 34). Jewish society lacks such great leaders. Jesus's referral of himself as a good shepherd is not an accident: "I am the good shepherd; the good shepherd lays down his life for the sheep" (John 10:11).

Unlike Luke, who emphasizes the importance of repentance, Matthew advances the importance of "these little ones" who are lost (Mt 18:14). "These little ones" could be marginalized people in Jewish society and beyond it. From Matthew's perspective, they could be any people who need God's care and his justice. Severe consequences will follow if people do not serve or feed those vulnerable people as we see in the final judgment scene in Matthew 25.

Questions for Reflection/Discussion

1. What are qualifications for the good shepherd? Share your experience of losing something or someone in the family/community.
2. How can we distinguish a good shepherd from a bad shepherd?
3. If a member is led astray or lost, whose responsibility is that: a shepherd, a sheep, or both?

Entrusted Money

MATTHEW 25:14-30

14 "For it is as if a man, going on a journey, summoned his slaves and entrusted his property to them; 15 to one he gave five talents, to another two, to another one, to each according to his ability. Then he went away. 16 The one who had received the five talents went off at once and traded with them, and made five more talents. 17 In the same way, the one who had the two talents made two more talents. 18 But the one who had received the one talent went off and dug a hole in the ground and hid his master's money. 19 After a long time the master of those slaves came and settled accounts with them. 20 Then the one who had received the five talents came forward, bringing five more talents, saying, 'Master, you handed over to me five talents; see, I have made five more talents.' 21 His master said to him, 'Well done, good and trustworthy slave; you have been trustworthy in a few things, I will put you in charge of many things; enter into the joy of your master.' 22 And the one with the two talents also came forward, saying, 'Master, you handed over to me two talents; see, I have made two more talents.' 23 His master said to him, 'Well done, good and trustworthy slave; you have been trustworthy in a few things, I will put you in charge of many things; enter into the joy of your master.' 24 Then the one who had received the one talent also came forward, saying, 'Master, I knew that you were a harsh man, reaping where you did not sow, and gathering where you did not scatter seed; 25 so I was afraid, and I went and hid your talent in the ground. Here you have what is yours.' 26 But his master replied, 'You wicked and lazy slave! You knew, did you, that I reap where I did not sow, and gather where I did not scatter? 27 Then you ought to have invested my money with the bankers, and on my return I would have received what was my own with interest. 28 So take the talent from him, and give it to the one with the ten talents. 29 *For to all those who have, more will be given, and they will have an abundance; but from those who have nothing, even*

what they have will be taken away. *30 As for this worthless slave, throw him into the outer darkness, where there will be weeping and gnashing of teeth.'* [Italics indicate the Matthean redaction]

The parable of talents is found in Matthew 25:14-30 and Luke 19:11-28. But the two versions of this parable are very different with each other. Both the Matthean and Lukan versions of this parable underwent changes because of the evangelists' theological concerns. However, the Matthean version (except for 25:29-30) seems to get closer to the original parable of Jesus because Matthew, unlike Luke, does not incorporate the theme of eschatology and kingly master (Lk 19:12). It also must be pointed out that both Matthew and Luke add their interpretation to this parable: Mt 25: 29-30 and Lk 19:25-27, respectively. This part of the evangelists' redaction should be cut off from the original form of the parable. Otherwise, understanding of this parable will be so confusing or difficult.

In Matthew, the master gives out the different amount of money (5 talents, 2 talents, and 1 talent, which is a gold coin, equivalent to 6,000 denarii, wage of 16-year work) according to the slaves' ability. But in Luke, he gives the same small amount of money (10 minas, equivalent to 1,000 denarii, and worth of 30-month wage) to the slaves and commands them to do business. Also, the master in Luke tells his slaves he will return. The Lukan focus is discipleship and eschatology. Until the master returns, they have to make a profit (Lk 19:13). But in Matthew, the master does not say whether he will return or not. Rather, he acts as if he would not return, entrusting his entire property to his slaves according to their abilities.

In Matthew, the master entrusts his property to his slaves and gives out five talents, two talents, and one talent, respectively, according to their abilities. One talent is 6000 denarii, and one denarion (silver coin) is a usual daily wage. In today' term, one talent is equivalent to at least about a half million dollars (for 16 years work). So the master's total asset (8 talents) amounts to about four million dollars. All this suggests that slaves are entrusted with large money.[11] The master is supposed to know each slave's ability and work performance. Based on this information, the master entrusts his property to them by their ability. So his decision must be trustable. The master also knows that each slave's ability is limited; not all of them have the same ability. Some can do more than others. That is a reality the master knows. The master's decision provides the ideal condition for his slaves. It is a win-win policy. Here each person's ability is big enough to take half million dollars. Ability may mean several things: intellect, health, and various gifts of life such as communication skill or power of empathy. Nobody can say, "I have no ability." All are given abilities or gifts of God though

---

11. What the talents represent has been the issue of debate and the seed of diverse interpretation. Usually, they have something to do with gifts and abilities of persons that require "fidelity in all that God has entrusted to us." See Adolf Jülicher, *Die Gleichnisreden Jesu*, 481: "auf Treue in allem, was Gott uns anvertraut hat." Classical examples of this line of thought include Chrysostom and Calvin: "each person's ability, whether in the way of protection, or in money, or in teaching, or whatever" (Chrysostom) and the gifts of God (Calvin). See Chrysostom's Homily LXXVIII in St. John Chrysostom, *Homilies on Matthew* in *Nicene and Post-Nicene Fathers* Vol. 10 (Grand Rapids: Eerdmans, 1978): 472; John Calvin, *Commentary on a Harmony of the Evangelists: Matthew, Mark, and Luke* Vol. 3 (Edinburgh: Calvin Translation Society, 1846): 444. With contemporary scholars the issue takes us to go further in similar and yet different directions; for J. Jeremias, they are the Word of God, for John Carpenter, "faithfulness of endeavor"; for A. M. Hunter, "a natural gift"; for Hultgren, faithfulness in the use of gifts; for Bernard Scott, bold action; for Davies and Dale Allison, responsibility of disciples. See Joachim Jeremias, *The Parables of Jesus* (London: SCM, 1963): 61-62; John B. Carpenter, "The Parable of the Talents in Missionary Perspective: A Call for an Economic Spirituality," *Missiology* 25 (1997): 167; A. M. Hunter, *The Parables of Then and Now*, London: SCM, 1971), 96-97; A. J. Hultgren, *The Parables of Jesus: A Commentary* (Grand Rapids: Eerdmans, 2000), 278-279; Bernard Scott, *Hear the Parable: A Commentary on the Parables of Jesus* (Minneapolis, MN: Fortress, 1989), 234; Davies and Dale Allison, *A Critical and Exegetical Commentary on the Gospel According to Matthew*, Vol. 3 (London: T & T Clark, 1997), 402-403. In the end, it is worth hearing Don Carson's comment about the identification of the talents: "Attempts to identify the talents with spiritual gifts, the law, natural endowments, the gospel, or whatever else, lead to a narrowing of the parable with which Jesus would have been uncomfortable. Perhaps he chose the talent or mina symbolism because of its capacity for varied application." See D. A. Carson, "Matthew," in *The Expositor's Bible Commentary*, vol. 8 (ed. Frank E. Gaebelein; Grand Rapids: Zondervan, 1984), 516.

to a different degree. However, the master does not say what to do with that money. Good slaves are supposed to know what they have to do given the trust by their master. Otherwise, they are not instructed about what to do with the money. They must decide what to do with their responsibility. So the one who received five talents and two talents doubled what they received. They did their best given their ability. Here the point of the parable is not how much they earned but how much efforts they put. But the one who received one talent acts differently from the other two slaves.[12] He hid it in a hole in the ground. He looks smart in hiding one talent so that he will lose nothing. He expects that his master cannot make him hold accountable for the entrusted money.

Some time later the master returns and checks about his property. Those who received the five talents and two talents are praised because of their hard work. They were not told to make a profit, but they knew what their master wanted. The point is not that they doubled the received money but that they worked hard. Would the master punish these two slaves if they made no profit after many efforts? The answer will be no, based on his response to the slave given one talent who says his master would punish him if he makes no profit. The master is seen by this slave as a harsh master in society. Out of this fear, he said he hid the one talent without even trying to do something. This slave's problem is two-fold: One he misjudges his master; the other that he does nothing other than hiding it in a hole (the very different act of hiding unlikely in the parable of leaven where a woman hides leaven in flour). First, the master corrects this slave's understanding about himself, saying: "You wicked and lazy slave! You knew, did you, that I reap where I did not sow, and gather where I did not scatter?" (Mt 25:26). The

---

12. Some read this parable allegorically or from Matthew's perspective. A. M. Hunter argues that the third slave represents "the religious leaders of Israel." For Daniel Harrington the third slave represents Jewish opponents of Matthew's community. But I read this story as metaphor. See A.M. Hunter, *The Parables of Then and Now*, 97; Daniel Harrington, *The Gospel of Matthew*, Collegeville, MN: Liturgical Press, 1991, 354. Similarly, see Lane McGaughy, "The Fear of Yahweh and the Mission of Judaism: A Postexilic Maxim and Its Early Christian Expansion in the Parable of the Talents," *JBL* 94.2 (1975) 235-245.

master underlines hard work and trial in the sense that no one can expect harvest without sowing.

Second, because of his misunderstanding about the master, this slave wastes the opportunity of doing great work with one talent (half million dollars). In economic theory, there is a term called "opportunity cost," which means "the opportunities forgone in the choice of one expenditure over others."[13] In this slave's case, he did nothing other than keeping it in a hole. However, his act results in a huge loss of an economic opportunity that could do great works for the world. His mistake is that he saw the one talent only without thinking about its positive use. That is why the master scolds this slave who did nothing. Otherwise, he is not punished because he made no profit. Because of his selfish, fear-driven act, the world loses the opportunity of investment. So, the social cost is involved here, which means the value of the one talent was not kept.[14]

In conclusion, some read the master in this parable as a cruel master who exploits his slaves at the same time viewing the third slave as a hero who willfully resists his master not by making a profit for him. But this reading is stretched, as we saw before

13. http://www.britannica.com/EBchecked/topic/430254/opportunity-cost. Accessed on July 20, 2016.

14. There is another strand of interpretation about this parable, which is exactly the opposite of my interpretation. In it, the master in this parable represents an abusive, exploitive master, and it is the third slave who is "the model for Christians" because he resists the evil master's economic exploitation. See Justin Ukpong, "The Parable of the Talents (Matt 25:14-30): Commendation or Critique of Exploitation?: A Social-Historical and Theological Reading." *Neotestamenica* 46.1 (2012), 205 (190-207). His interpretation follows Richard Rohrbaugh, William Herzog, and Luise Schottroff, who, more or less, read this parable as critique of economic exploitation, against its social world where there is no economic justice. Since we do not know Jesus's intention or mind, this reading is not impossible. See Richard Rohrbaugh, "A Peasant Reading of the Talents/Pounds: A Text of Terror?"; William Herzog, *Parables as Subversive Speech: Jesus as Pedagogue of the Oppressed* (Louisville, KY: W/JKP, 1994); Luise Schottroff, *The Parables of Jesus* (Minneapolis: Fortress, 2006). In contrast, Warren Carter's reading is nuanced; in it, he argues that Matthew mimics the imperial culture in ways that the Matthean Jesus appears as the master to emphasize faithful discipleship. See Warren Carter, *Matthew and the Margins: A Socio-Political and Religious Reading* (Sheffield: Sheffield Academic Press, 2000), 487-488.

because the master's point is not about the earned profit but the slave's work ethic; that is, he did not even try to do something with such much money. Otherwise, the point of this parable is not about challenging the malpractice of hiring and pay. The point is how each person can do his or her best given the grace and gifts of God. The funny thing here is that the third slave hides the one talent in a hole in the ground, which is the place for the seed. Money should not be placed there. What is to be hidden and planted in the ground is not the money but the seed, which has to die to produce grain.

If the master is compared to God, we can get the lesson that God is to be both feared and trusted. Fear of God is not a passive stance he or she does not even try, but it is his/her diligent work. A fear-driven lifestyle is discouraged because there is always enough grace of God.

Matthew thinks that members of the Christian community are given the same call but given the different gifts of God. That is why in Matthew's version, the servants receive different amounts of money: five talents, two talents, and one talent. Once given the talent, each must work hard to bear fruit. The desirable work ethic in the work of the kingdom is not fear but courage. The courage that God will be with them under any circumstances is the faith of the Matthean community. Also, each person must know that he/she is given the enormous gift from God; even one talent is huge money. God's grace for each person is too great to pay back. However, they have to do their best in kingdom work with a sense of great honor and responsibility.

Questions for Reflection/Discussion

1. In Matthew, the master entrusts his entire property to his slaves according to their abilities. What does this act of the master imply in the rule of God? What is a different ability?

2. In Luke, the master gives out the same money to the slaves. What does this act of the master imply in the rule of God?

Jesus's Truth

Does this same amount of money have to do with Lukan theology? (Treating all the same? Receiving the same mission of God? etc).

4

Matthean Unique Parables

Wheat and Weed

MATTHEW 13:24-30
24 He put before them another parable: "The kingdom of heaven may be compared to someone who sowed good seed in his field; 25 *but while everybody was asleep, an enemy came and sowed weeds among the wheat, and then went away.* 26 So when the plants came up and bore grain, then the weeds appeared as well. 27 *And the slaves of the householder came and said to him, 'Master, did you not sow good seed in your field? Where, then, did these weeds come from?'* 28 He answered, 'An enemy has done this.' The slaves said to him, 'Then do you want us to go and gather them?' 29 But he replied, 'No; for in gathering the weeds you would uproot the wheat along with them. 30 Let both of them grow together until the harvest; and at harvest time I will tell the reapers, Collect the weeds first and bind them in bundles to be burned, but gather the wheat into my barn.'" [Italics indicate Matthew's redaction]

THIS PARABLE IS UNIQUE to Matthew and it is also found in the Gospel of Thomas. According to John Meier, Thomas version of this parable may be a radical abbreviation of Matthew's version.[1] For example, individual words and phrases in Thomas reflect Matthew's text of the parable: "the kingdom of the Father" rephrasing "the kingdom of heaven" in Matthew. Apparently, this parable in Matthew 13:24-30 has an allegorical interpretation in 13:36-43, which is Matthew's interpretation. We have seen before the evangelists' allegorical interpretation of the parable of the sower. Now the question is whether the whole text in the parable proper (Matt 13:24-30) comes from Jesus. Scholars have different opinions about the boundary of the original parable: Kingsbury reading 24b-26 as original; Schweizer, 24b, 26, 28b-29 as original; Weder, 24b, 26, 30b as the original.[2] It seems that Schweizer's view is close to the original form since Jesus does not allegorize his parable. The references about an enemy (v.25, 28) and separation of wheat and weeds (v.30) come from Matthew as we see in his allegorical interpretation (v.36-43).

While the parable of the sower assumes that the seeds are excellent quality, the parable of the wheat and weeds introduces a new reality in the field (world) that there are bad "weed seeds" sown together with good seeds.[3] It is natural that the field has both the wheat and weeds. In this situation, the realistic question is what to do with the weeds among the wheat. Is it better to remove them now than later at the harvest? Likewise, the question is how to deal with the coexistence of good and evil in the community or society. Surprisingly, that coexistence also resides in one's heart.

Apparently, someone sows only good seeds in his field, but later servants find that weeds also grow together with the plants (13:24b, 26). So they report to the householder, asking, "Then do you want us to go and gather them?" (13:28b). But the master

---

1. For more about this, see John Meier, "The Parable of the Wheat and the Weeds (Matthew 13:24-30): Is *Thomas's* Version (Logion 57) Independent?" *JBL* 131, no. 4 (2012): 715-732.

2. Jack Kingsbury, *Parables* (SPCK, 1969), 65. E. Schweizer, *The Good News According to Matthew* (WJKP, 1975), 303. Hans Weder, *Die Gleichnisse Jesu als Metaphern*, FRLANT 120, 3rd ed. Göttingen, 1984.

3. William Doty, "An Interpretation: Parable of the Weeds and Wheat," *Interpretation* 25.2 (1971) 185-193.

replies, "No; for in gathering the weeds you would uproot the wheat along with them" (13:29). Jesus's point is what to do with the existence of the weeds. Otherwise, he is not talking about the origin of the weeds; rather, it is Matthew who connects the weeds with the enemy.[4] The weeds are simply there; that is a reality in farming. Given this reality, what is the best option to deal with the weeds? Common wisdom in this time says: the earlier the weeds are removed, the better for the plants. But the master asks his servants to leave them alone. The reason is the wheat can be hurt. Actually, the master's instruction is very unrealistic and costly because the poisonous weeds can contaminate the grain of wheat. Moreover, at the harvest, the work of separation would not be easy because the weeds are big enough. Smart farmers will want to remove the weeds as early as possible. In fact, the experienced servants can discern the weeds (darnel) by the size of leaves.

God's rule requires new attitudes toward others (or enemies). First, God's rule must embrace both good and bad in the community or in society. A rigid division between the sacred and the profane is unhelpful in the rule of God because God's impartial love cannot be realized by separation of the enemy. Given that reality of a mixed community or of a mixture of good and evil even within a person's mind, what we need is an active mind that we can influence others in a good way. In that sense, the teaching of this parable is similar to Jesus's command: "Love your enemies and pray for those who persecute you" (Mt 5:44). In the Sermon on the Mount, Jesus continues to say: "for he makes his sun rise on the evil and on the good, and sends rain on the righteous and on the unrighteous. For if you love those who love you, what reward do you have? ... Be perfect, therefore, as your heavenly Father is perfect" (Mt 5:45-48). Plants' growing together with weeds are uneasy. But perhaps the existence of weeds may help the community or people to maintain a healthy spirituality. Jesus is not so much

---

4. For the role of this parable in Matthew's theology, see Robert McIver, "The parable of the weeds among the wheat (Matt 13:24-30, 36-43) and the relationship between the kingdom and the church as portrayed in the Gospel of Matthew," *JBL* 114.4 (1995) 643-659.

interested in the final judgment of "bad" people as Matthew allegorizes his parable.

The ultimate vision for God's children is to be perfect like God. God wants all, good and evil, to live in peace and justice. Moreover, weeds are everywhere; they are within a good person's mind too. So we should inspect ourselves first before looking at evil in others. Oftentimes people are hasty judging others without observing their own faults. It seems that Jesus and Paul differ from each other in their dealing with evil or weeds. Paul is adamant about the community's unity and purity (1 Cor 5:1-13). Paul's advice to evil doers in the community is to expel them so that the community may remain uncorrupted. It is understandable that Paul is so much concerned about the newly formed community's identity and union. He, as a movement follower, community organizer, and practical theologian, had anxieties about the newly converted communities. But Jesus is an idealist or visionary who has confidence about God's power that will be effective to all, good and bad. Jesus does not deal with one particular community as Paul did. Jesus is rather a movement leader who is concerned with all people.

Questions for Reflection/Discussion

1. What are good seeds and weeds in the rule of God? What is the best policy to deal with this issue of coexistence of good and evil in the community?
2. What does the field represent in this parable?
3. In a way, Jesus is more optimistic about human transformation than Paul. What do you think?

Treasure

MATTHEW 13:44
The kingdom of heaven is like treasure hidden in a field, which someone found and hid; then in his joy he goes and sells all that he has and buys that field.

GOS.THOM109
Jesus said, The (Father's) kingdom is like a person who had a treasure hidden in his field but did not know it. And [when] he died he left it to his [son]. The son [did] not know about it either. He took over the field and sold it. The buyer went plowing, [discovered] the treasure, and began to lend money at interest to whomever he wished.

A treasure parable appears in Matthew 13:44 and the Gospel of Thomas 109. However, the difference between them is big. Whereas the former compares God's rule with treasure, the latter compares with a person. Besides, Thomas's version is longer than Matthew with more details about treasure and people involved (father, son, and the buyer, lenders). Thomas elaborates Matthew's version or the earlier form of the parable to stress a person's effort to gain treasure—represented by knowledge. In Thomas, the buyer lends money at interest to buy the treasure, which shows Thomas's efforts for discipleship. In Matthew, however, the person sells what he has. Overall, Matthew's version seems closer to the original parable of Jesus than Thomas.

The ancient practice of hiding treasure in a field is a way of securing wealth in times of crisis.[5] Then sometimes people who buried it forgot about it and it could be discovered later. However, from this parable, we do not know what exactly happened to the treasures or people involved. We do not know who buried it, who found it, or how it was discovered. One thing we know is that treasure is discovered unexpectedly. At the time of discovery, what does this person do? That person who finds treasure sells all he has

---

5. Barbara Reid, *Parables for Preachers*, Year A, 120.

to buy the field. Unlikely Thomas, Matthew suggests the person is rich enough to buy the field.

Now the issue is about entitlement: Is he legally right to do so? According to the Talmud, a person in this parable must seek the owner of the field because treasure does not belong to him.[6] This understanding of the Talmud is based on the common sense of ethical duty. To follow this line of ethics, even if the owner of the field is unidentified, still the issue remains about entitlement. In a similar context, with the newly purchased land, the treasure still belongs to the previous owner. Only after seven years if the owner cannot be found, then the treasure belongs to the new owner.[7] Therefore, some scholars think that the person who finds treasure is dishonest because he does not return it to the owner.[8] There are no attempts to find the owner. But Jesus's point is not of legal issues as seen above, but in the aspect of God's rule suddenly revealed, as a hidden treasure is discovered all of sudden. It means that a person does not control God's rule. When treasure is revealed, there must be a quick, radical decision about it.

Like hidden treasure, God's rule is precious and yet difficult to find. People do not search for it. Even if the treasure is found, it must be obtained by purchase. The precious rule of God is not free but requires a cost. Jesus preaches that in Mark 1:15: For God's rule to be effective, people must change their mind (*metanoia*).

In Matthew's community, all are called to the work of God because of the Messiah's exemplary life and faith in God. The calling of God must be a decisive moment for them; when called by God, they cannot delay such a call. There is a time to hear God's good news and there is a time to respond. The parable of Treasure echoes such a teaching of Matthew that the opportunity is given suddenly and that it must be taken immediately. As a person in the parable discovers treasures hidden in a field and acts on

---

6. J. Duncan M. Derrett, "Law in the New Testament: The Treasure in the Field," *ZNW* 54 (1963) 31-42.

7. Bernard B. Scott, "Lost Junk, Found Treasure," *TBT* 26 (1988) 31-34.

8. Barbara Reid, *Parables for Preachers* Year A, 122-3.

it immediately to make it the most, the kingdom people in the Matthean community must be similar to that.

Questions for Reflection/Discussion

1. What is the meaning of the treasure hidden in a field? Why is it hidden?
2. Is treasure found by accident or by purpose or in the middle of doing something?
3. Is this parable problematic from an ethical perspective because the one who finds treasure hides it without reporting to the owner of the field?

Pearl

> MATT 13:45-46
> 45 Again, the kingdom of heaven is like a merchant in search of fine pearls; 46 on finding one pearl of great value, he went and sold all that he had and bought it.

> THOM 76:1
> 1 Jesus said, The Father's kingdom is like a merchant who had a supply of merchandise and found a pearl. That merchant was prudent; he sold the merchandise and bought the single pearl for himself.

Matthew and Thomas edited the source parable in different directions. Matthew's version has more of a natural flow of the story than Thomas's. In Matthew, the merchant is in search of fine pearls and finds one pearl of great value and sells everything to buy it. Thomas lacks such a smooth flow of the story; instead, the merchant looks for one pearl from beginning to ending.

While in the parable of treasure God's rule is compared with treasure hidden in a field, in the Pearl it is compared with a merchant.[9] This merchant actively seeks fine pearls, which is contrasted with the parable of treasure.[10] Finding one pearl of great price, he invests all in it. This merchant seems strange because he sells all to buy a single pearl. This general practice of merchants seeks more profits by buying and selling lots of fine pearls.

Because of this finding and all investment, the merchant's destiny also changes. This merchant needs not search for pearl any longer because he has the best one now. One pearl of great price is kept and cannot be resold.[11] The most valuable thing cannot be resold because it is irreplaceable with any other. If this merchant finds the most valuable pearl in his eyes and sells all to buy it, it must be priceless and too valuable to be resold. Such a great pearl cannot be resold because one cannot live without it. Perhaps it will not be as valuable as other merchants think. Nobody can sell the most precious. If someone enters a ministry by quitting his/her job and studying at a seminary, the ministry is a great pearl to him/her, which cannot be given up for whatever. All is invested because ministry is a great pearl. If that person leaves the ministry to make more money, that is the evidence that ministry is not his/her pearl of great value. As we see here, the merchant's identity changes because of his/her discovery of a great pearl. The merchant is no more a seeker of pearls because he already owns the best pearl. He/she will not resell it because it is too valuable to give up.

Once in the community of God, the members of the Matthean community must commit to the good news of God as Jesus showed his faith. That is a matter of discipleship in Matthew. So the parable of Pearl contributes to that discipleship. Pearl represents Christian vocation for God. Nothing is more important to the kingdom of God than the full commitment to the work of God. Wherever they go or whatever they do, their primary task is to do

---

9. Given the image of merchants in the Scripture, which is generally negative (Sir 26:20; Isa 23:8; Ezek 27; 1 Tim 2:9; Rev 17:4; 18:15-16), the merchant in this parable seems strange and does not act according to the general rule of business: to buy more of the fine pearls and to sell them later with more profits.

10. Barbara Reid, *Parables for Preachers*, Year A, 124.

11. Amy-Jill Levine, *Short Stories by Jesus: The Enigmatic Parables of a Controversial Rabbi* (New York: HarperCollins, 2014), 136-150.

the work of God. Each person's pearl may be different because not all do the same work for God.

Questions for Reflection/Discussion

1. Do you think the merchant bought a pearl of great price to resell it and gain more profits?
2. What do you think about this statement: "The most precious thing cannot be resold?"
3. What is your pearl of great price without which you cannot live?

Vineyard Workers

MATTHEW 20:1-16

1 "For the kingdom of heaven is like a landowner who went out early in the morning to hire laborers for his vineyard. 2 After agreeing with the laborers for the usual daily wage, he sent them into his vineyard. 3 When he went out about nine o'clock, he saw others standing idle in the marketplace; 4 and he said to them, 'You also go into the vineyard, and I will pay you what is right or just.' So they went. 5 When he went out again about noon and about three o'clock, he did the same. 6 And about five o'clock he went out and found others standing around; and he said to them, 'Why are you standing here idle all day?' 7 They said to him, 'Because no one has hired us.' He said to them, 'You also go into the vineyard.' 8 When evening came, the owner of the vineyard said to his manager, 'Call the laborers and give them their pay, beginning with the last and then going to the first.' 9 When those hired about five o'clock came, each of them received the usual daily wage. 10 Now when the first came, they thought they would receive more; but each of them also received the usual daily wage. 11 And when they received it, they grumbled against the landowner, 12

saying, 'These last worked only one hour, and you have made them equal to us who have borne the burden of the day and the scorching heat.' 13 But he replied to one of them, 'Friend, I am doing you no wrong; did you not agree with me for the usual daily wage? 14 Take what belongs to you and go; I choose to give to this last the same as I give to you. 15 Am I not allowed to do what I choose with what belongs to me? Or are you envious because I am good (*agathos*)?' 16 So the last will be first, and the first will be last."

This parable is unique to Matthew and must be genuine to Jesus. There are no important textual issues other than a few translation matters: *ek denariou ten hemeran* (v. 2 and 10), *ho ean ei dikaion* (v.4), and *agathos* (v. 15). *Ek denariou ten hemeran* means "one denarius a day," which is the usual daily wage. So the NRSV translates it as "the usual daily wage." *Ho ean ei dikaion* means "whatever is right or just." The NJB translates it as "a fair wage," which is not a good one because it conveys no direct sense of justice (*dikaios*). *Dikaios* is an adjective which has to do with justice or righteousness. So the NRSV and NIV translate it as "whatever is right." But from the economic justice perspective, a better translation would be "whatever is just," which may emphasize the importance of justice to those who joined the vineyard late. *Agathos* plainly means "good" rather than "generous," which is adopted by the NRSV and NIV. But the NKJ correctly picks up a sense meant by this parable in which the point is the character of good for this master, not merely that of generosity. We will see all about these in our interpretation below.

This parable deals with economic justice in God's rule. Justice or righteousness[12] is one of the most important themes in the

12. Both justice and righteousness appear frequently in the Hebrew Bible, and oftentimes they are interchangeable. Justice (*mishpat* in Hebrew) has more to do with economic justice. Righteousness (*tsedaqah* in Hebrew) has more to do with God's character and action. The adjective *tsaddiq* often applies to God's character: "The Rock, his work is perfect, and all his ways are just. A faithful God, without deceit, just and upright is he" (Deut 32:4; see also Ps 129:4; 145:17; Job 34:17). *Tsaddiq* also applies to God's action in terms of redemption (Isa 45:21; Ps 116:5) and promises (Neh 9:8). Then, by and large, *mishpat*

Matthean Unique Parables

Hebrew Bible, and Jesus continues that tradition.[13] In Matthew Jesus appears as the Jewish Messiah, who fulfills the scriptures. Jesus wants his baptism so he may fulfill the righteousness (Mt 3:13-17), and in the Sermon on the Mount, he says he came to fulfill the law and the prophets (Mt 5:17). In Matthew 6:33, Jesus combines God's rule with his righteousness: "But strive first for the kingdom of God and his righteousness and all these things will be given to you as well."[14] This picture of the Matthean Jesus is close to

---

(justice) has to be the result of human lives because of God's righteousness. When this tradition about justice/righteousness comes to Jesus and Paul, they also stand with that. For example, Paul emphasizes "the righteousness of God," which is God's own righteousness (his character and action) as in Rom 3:21-26. Jesus also emphasizes God's rule and his righteousness (Mt 6:33). As God is holy, people are asked to be holy, seeking justice in matters of human lives. But when it goes further down to Deutero-Pauline, Pastorals, and later epistles in the New Testament, the meaning of righteousness changes and applies to believers ("one is justified once and for all"). In fact, linguistically speaking, the conveyance of the Hebrew meaning of these two different words (*mishpat* and *tsaddiq*) must be pessimistic because Greek does not have separate words for these. Both of these Hebrew terms are translated as *dikaosyne* (justice, judgment, righteousness).

13. In particular, the eighth century BCE prophets such as Isaiah, Amos, and Micah communicate the importance of justice of God with people who do not follow the way of God—the way of righteousness and justice. Righteousness has more to do with God's character and covenantal action toward his people in times of crisis, whether by internal conflict or corruption or by external oppression by foreign armies. Prophets criticize Jewish leaders because they do not seek God's righteousness. God is the one who is righteous, and people have to be like him in all their lives. As God is perfect, they are to be like that too. Now justice has more to do with the result of God's righteousness in this world. For example, there must be fair redistribution of wealth and means of life among the people. Economic justice is part of this.

14. This parable can be read along with Matthew 6:25-34 where Jesus talks about God's rule and his righteousness (*dikaiosyne*). What is the teaching of Matthew 6:33? Does it say that "if you seek the kingdom of God first, all things will be given to you"? Is this a matter of God first and the rest will be given? The problem of this reading is twofold. First, this is very individualistic reading that does not consider the importance of community. Second, there is a dualism between God's kingdom and individual personal work. But from the perspective of justice and community, as we see in the Vineyard Laborers, the meaning of 6:33 should be different from such a traditional reading. The key to this reading is the verb *prostithemi*, which means "to proceed." If God's rule is

57

the historical Jesus, who continues with the Jewish tradition about God of justice and righteousness.

So in the Vineyard Laborers, Jesus raises questions about justice/righteousness,[15] which means "rightness" in human lives. The landlord in the parable promises to pay "what is right or just (*ho dikaios*)" in 20:4. If God's rule is effective in the matters of economic life, what has to be changed? What is the right vision of an economy in God's rule? What is the acceptable spirit of labor in the vineyard? Therefore, we should not read this parable as an allegory of salvation in ways the early hired in the morning are Jews while the late-hired in the afternoon are Gentiles.

Full Employment

There are a few metaphors in this parable: vineyard owner, vineyard, laborers, labor market, and wage. Among these, the vineyard owner is a key to interpreting this parable. He is unlike a typical master who is not concerned about full employment or the need of the less fortunate. Though some scholars see this owner as an evil master who exploits his laborers in ways that make them compete while paying not enough to all, Jesus seems not to focus on that problem.[16] David Buttrick says the owner is "unjust

---

pursued in community, members of the community will live according to that rule. Then, all things will proceed abundantly to all. A community of justice is possible only when people seek God's rule wholeheartedly.

15. In Matthew the term *dikaiosyne* (righteousness or justice) occurs seven times: 3:15; 5:6, 10, 20; 6:1, 33; 21:32. It occurs only once in Luke, twice in John, and not at all in Mark. All this implies that Matthew portrays Jesus as a Jewish Messiah who fulfills the scriptures. Its adjective form *dikaios* also appears sixteenth times in Matthew whereas it occurs only twice in Mark; eleven times in Luke, and three times in John. *Dikaios* in Matthew is in the following verses: 1:19; 5:45; 9:13; 10:41; 13:17, 54, 59; 20:4; 23:28, 29, 35; 25:37, 46; 27:4, 19, 24.

16. Among these scholars who view the vineyard owner as a bad tyrant are William Herzog and David Buttrick. William Herzog, *Parables as Subversive Speech: Jesus as Pedagogue of the Oppressed* (Louisville, KY: WJKP, 1994), 94-96. See David Buttrick, *Speaking Parables: A Homiletic Guide* (Louisville, KY: WJKP, 2000), 114.

and arrogant,"[17] and William Loader says, "The scene is now not only one of exploitation but also of arbitrariness and injustice."[18] Similarly, Herzog believes that the owner is bad and tactic enough to block union labors, so to speak. But *oikodespotes* (translated as "landowner") in 16:1 may not be so negative a term because the term means a landowner, master of the house, or owner of the house, which is not used negatively in Matthew 13:27 or 21:33. More than that, we see an atypical image of the vineyard owner here in this parable, who is concerned with full employment and adequate pay to the laborers.[19] The landlord goes out to seek laborers five times.[20] This practice must be unusual because he could find the enough number of laborers one or two times. But his last time going out is five o'clock in the afternoon. Also, he goes out to hire people. Healthy or sick, old or young, they all are employed. We also have to know the late-hired people were not lazy but jobless (*argos* in vv. 3, 6, as "without works") at the time.[21] They clearly

17. David Buttrick, *Speaking Parables: A Homiletic Guide* (Louisville, KY: WJKP, 2000), 114.

18. William Loader, "First Thoughts on Passages from Matthew in the Lectionary," http://wwwstaff.murdoch.edu.au/~loader/MtPent14.htm. Accessed on May 8, 2015.

19. Amy-Jill Levine, *Short Stories by Jesus: The Enigmatic Parables of a Controversial Rabbi* (New York, NY: HarperOne, 2014), 197-219.

20. Referring to the hours of the parable, Origen allegorically interprets that the five hours represent five periods in the history of the world and matches the five human senses to these periods. Namely: the sense of touch with the first period, Adam and Eve; the sense of smell with Noah; the sense of hearing with Moses and the sense of the eye-sight with the people after Christ. See *Commentaius in Matthaeum* XV, 30 ed. E. Klostermann, *GCS* 10, 441-448. Augustine similarly does so and yet exhorts his audience to live with full devotion to Christ before too late. See his Sermon 37. For more about patristic interpretation about the hours of the parable, see J. M. Tevel, "The Laborers in the Vineyard: the Exegesis of Matthew 20:1-7 in the Early Church," *Vigiliae Christianae* 46 (1992) 356-380.

21. Hispanic interpreters read the lastly hired people as those who are marginalized and deprived of equal opportunities for work. I agree with their interpretation. For example, see Pablo A. Jiménez, "The Laborers of the Vineyard (Matthew 20:1-16): A Hispanic Homiletical Reading," *Journal for Preachers* 21.1 (1997) 35-40. See also Justo L González, *Tres meses en la escuela de Mateo* (Nashville Abingdon Press, 1996), 118-119; José D Rodríguez,

say their unemployment is because nobody hired them. All they want is a work and relevant pay.

The Usual Daily Wage

The vineyard owner is concerned about the need for everyday people who need daily bread. Levine observes: "The point is not that those who have 'get more,' but that those who have not 'get enough.'"[22] As pay time is near, all laborers wait for their wage, which is the usual daily wage. But when those who joined the vineyard late in the afternoon receive one denarion, those who came early in the morning expect to receive more, forgetting about the promised wage and neglecting to see the need of the rest who have to feed their families. But they also receive the same one denarion and complain to the master, "like the grumbling of the Israelites in the desert" (Exod 17:3; Num 11:1; 14:27, 29). However, this complaint is actually groundless from a legal perspective because they were contracted with one denarion, which is the usual daily wage—"what is just" (16:4) and proper to their daily living wage.[23] Here the problem is these early comers do not see the need of those others. From a critical perspective of the master, there is no guarantee these early comers produced more than the rest. The

---

"The Parable of the Affirmative-Action Employer," *Apuntes* 8.3 (1988) 51-59. Contra this kind of liberating interpretation for the lastly hired group, other scholars such as Joachim Jeremias and E. Schweizer comment negatively about the attitude of these laborers lastly hiried. Jeremias states: "Even if, in the case of the last labourers (sic) to be hired, it is their own fault that, in a time when the vineyard needs workers, they sit about in the marketplace gossiping till late afternoon; even if their excuse that no one has hired them (v. 7) is an idle evasion (like that of the servant in Matt. 25.24), a cover for their typical oriental indifference, yet they touch the owner's heart." See Joachim Jeremías, *The Parables of Jesus* (London: SCM, 1954), 26. Likewise, Schweizer observes: "it is evident they were not yet at the marketplace at the sixth or the ninth hour. It is simply left open whether their coming late to find work is their own fault." See E. Schweizer, *The Good News According to Matthew* (Louisville, KY: W/JKP, 1975), 392.

22. Levine, 218.
23. Ibid., 217-8.

amount of time invested may not be commensurate with the work. So it is hard to prove that the early comers worked more than the late comers. All are employed with the usual daily wage. This story is reminiscent of the manna story in Exodus 16:16: "This is what the LORD has commanded: 'Gather as much of it as each of you needs, an omer to a person according to the number of persons, all providing for those in their own tents.'"

Agathos (Good) as the Master's Character

The master rebuts the early comers' characterization that he is a dictator. The master says, "Am I not allowed to do what I choose with what belongs to me? Or are you envious because I am good (*agathos*)?" (16:15). Here *agathos* characterizes the master; he is good because he cares about economic justice for all and full employment. This character of "good" master is what we see in the righteousness of God in the Hebrew Bible. The base for the master's philosophy is that he followed the contract, which is based on economic justice for all. Eventually, he wants all to be employed with equal pay. Metaphorically speaking, the master is like God, who wants all his people to live in justice and peace in his creation. By extension, all people are to find work in his creation. All people must be fed in it, and that is economic justice envisioned in this parable. This kind of equal distribution of pay is found in 1 Sam 30:24-25 when David distributes the share of the spoil equally among those who go down to the battle and those who stay by the baggage (v.24).

Alternative Justice in God's Rule

This parable is concerned with a particular form of justice based on the need of people. This idea is close to the so-called "distributive justice." But there are also different kinds of justice: attributive, retributive, redemptive, and restorative. Attributive justice highlights a person's hard work, and so it must deserve a reward.

Retributive justice allows a just society by checking those who do wrong. Distributive justice is concerned with distributing wealth among different classes of people. Redemptive justice focuses on the recovery of those who are inflicted by personal or social tragedies. Last, restorative justice focuses on the equal starting point by which everybody has to start in their lives. All of these are important to God's rule, but this particular parable highlights the distributive justice.

In conclusion, this parable deals with economic justice about distributing income, full employment, and proper pay. One of the most serious problems in the neoliberal or capitalist economy is big wage disparity among classes or between genders. With this problem, another big challenge is the increasing number of contracted temporary workers who work like regular employees but do not get the full benefit. They belong to a third-party contractor and can be fired anytime. Hard or dangerous works are often given to a third-party contractor that sends its workers to the contracted original company. Delivery service of the post office is done with contractors that run with their delivery people. These employees do not belong to post office, and therefore, they are not paid enough and work under stress with inadequate pay. In nuclear plants or automobile factory, there are a good number of these kinds of the third-party-sent employees working under the instruction of the contracted company. They face the danger of unemployment and poor wage, plus that they do not expect various benefit packages. From the perspective of economic justice in God's rule, maximizing profit for the business or corporations should be checked; rather the focus must be on welfare of their employees. Jesus sees the need of everyday people. Otherwise, "Jesus is neither a Marxist nor a capitalist. Rather, he is both an idealist and a pragmatist."[24]

The parable of vineyard workers follows Matthew's thematic focus on the kingdom of God with God's righteousness or God's justice. God of the Hebrew Bible is the God of justice for all people. This parable supports that theme in ways that people in the world, no matter who they are, like vineyard workers, must be taken care

24. Amy-Jill Levine, *Short Stories*, 218.

of, not based on abilities but based on the need of their families. To push the gospel to the entire world, Matthew makes sure that all people are taken care of. This parable advocates the marginalized and stresses the importance of economic justice.

Questions for Reflection/Discussion

1. Do you agree this parable is about economic justice?
2. How can you evaluate the character of the landlord in this parable? Is he an exploitive master or the one concerned with justice?
3. What does vineyard represent in this parable?

Unmerciful Servant

MATTHEW 18:23-35
23 "For this reason the kingdom of heaven may be compared to a king who wished to settle accounts with his slaves. 24 When he began the reckoning, one who owed him ten thousand talents was brought to him; 25 and, as he could not pay, his lord ordered him to be sold, together with his wife and children and all his possessions, and payment to be made. 26 So the slave fell on his knees before him, saying, 'Have patience with me, and I will pay you everything.' 27 And out of pity for him, the lord of that slave released him and forgave him the debt. 28 But that same slave, as he went out, came upon one of his fellow slaves who owed him a hundred denarii; and seizing him by the throat, he said, 'Pay what you owe.' 29 Then his fellow slave fell down and pleaded with him, 'Have patience with me, and I will pay you.' 30 But he refused; then he went and threw him into prison until he would pay the debt. 31 When his fellow slaves saw what had happened, they were greatly distressed, and they went and reported to their lord all that had taken place. 32 Then his lord summoned him and said to him,

'You wicked slave! I forgave you all that debt because you pleaded with me. 33 Should you not have had mercy on your fellow slave, as I had mercy on you?' *34 And in anger his lord handed him over to be tortured until he would pay his entire debt. 35 So my heavenly Father will also do to every one of you, if you do not forgive your brother or sister from your heart."*

The parable of the unmerciful servant underwent heavy editing by Matthew. Mt 18:34-35 is Matthew's comment; that is, Matthew interprets Jesus's parable to teach the importance of forgiveness in the community, which is a continuation of community discourse in chapter 18. Matthew's comment on the consequence of this unforgiving slave is: "And in anger his lord handed him over to be tortured until he would pay his entire debt. So my heavenly Father will also do to every one of you, if you do not forgive your brother or sister from your heart" (18: 34-35). Scholars believe the 10,000 talents are an exaggeration made by Matthew, who wants to underline the incalculable size of God's mercy on members of the Christian community.[25] In the pre-Matthean form of the parable, the borrowed money is 10,000 denarii. But Matthew seems to have changed only one word here: from denarius to talents. But in Matthew's redaction, there is incongruence or conflict between the king's forgiveness to the slave and the master's judgment and punishment to him. This image of the king in the parable also has a conflict with Jesus's word in 18:21-22, where Jesus answers Peter that Peter must forgive the offender infinitely. So by removing Matthean redaction part, it is possible to have a close version of the early parable of Jesus, which deals with everyday life regarding economic life, especially in "the familiar world of masters and slaves, of debts and obligations to repay, i.e., of legal rights and claims."[26]

---

25. Josephus says that the whole Judean taxes for Rome per year was 600 talents only. The Roman general Pompey requested Judah to pay 10,000 talents to Rome. If 10,000 talents are an impossible amount to be repaid, then the slave's word of promise to repay seems empty words that express his fear. Josephus, *Ant.* 14.78; 17.319-20.

26. Martinus de Boer, 230.

Matthean Unique Parables

This parable proper is concerned with the need of mercy in a social space where people are entangled with various forms of debt-credit relations. By removing Matthean editing of the earlier parable, we can come up with the pre-Matthean parable:[27]

> A person wished to settle accounts with his servants. After he had begun reckoning, one debtor of 10,000 denarii was brought to him. And because he could not pay up, the master commanded him to be sold, with his wife and children and all that he had, and the sum to be repaid. So the servant fell down and was beseeching him, saying, "Be patient with me, and I shall repay you everything." And the master of that servant was moved with pity and released him and forgave him the loan.
>
> That servant found one of his fellow-servants, who owed him 100 denarii, and he grabbed and choked him, saying, "Pay up what you owe." So his fellow servant fell down and was beseeching him, saying, "Be patient with me, and I shall repay you." He did not wish to do so, but threw him into prison, until he should pay up what was owed.
>
> When his fellow servants saw what had happened, they were greatly shocked and reported to their master all that had happened. Then his master summoned him and said to him, "Evil servant, I forgave you all that debt since you beseeched me. Was it unnecessary also for you to have had mercy on your fellow-servant, as I had mercy on you?" And his master became angry and handed him over to the jailers until he should pay up all that was owed.

10,000 denarii—not 10,000 talents—is neither a small amount nor an impossible amount to repay. In Matthew's version 10,000 talents are the unrealistic number, but here the 10,000 denarii are the manageable amount in a real world. However, what surprises

---

27 The version that follows here is from Martinus de Boer, "Ten thousand talents: Matthew's interpretation and redaction of the parable of the Unforgiving Servant (Matt 18:23-35)," *CBQ* 50.2 (1988) 230 (214-232). See also J. D. Crossan, *In Parables. The Challenge of the Historical Jesus* (New York: Harper & Row, 1973) 108; Brandon Scott, "The king's accounting," 433-34.

Jesus's Truth

Jesus's audience is not the money but the master's unusual act of forgiveness of the debt, based on the servant's pleas. In usual social setting, the master will attempt to recover his lost money by selling the slave's property and family members. Given the value of a slave being 500 and 2,000 denarii,[28] 10,000 denarii are not too big a loan that cannot be repaid. So the servant makes a plea and asks for mercy. He asks for extending the due date, which is difficult in society. But the master listens to him and forgives his debt. In a familiar world where no mercy is expected, this slave finds mercy. That is a new world he never expected, but now here it is with him. That is a different world that God reigns.

After this, the slave goes out to the streets and meets one of his fellow slaves. But this time, he does not act like the one who forgave his debt. The money he lent is 100 denarii only. But this slave was harsh and merciless toward his fellow servant. Rejecting this poor fellow's realistic, genuine plea for the patience, this unmerciful servant puts him to jail and says he has to stay there until paying the debt in full. This poor slave must stay for his life because even the small debt of 100 denarii is such a huge debt that he cannot repay given his hopeless. This miserable slave could not say he would pay everything because 100 denarii is too big to pay back. He does not even know whether he could pay in full because he is out of business. So he does not utter empty words like the first slave but asks for patience. So possibly he collapsed when he met his creditor. There is a good contrast between them. Whereas the first slave was bold enough to ask for the master's patience with a good gesture of "kneeling down" (*prosykuneo*) (18:26), which seems like a calculated act to acquire mercy, "his fellow slave *fell down* (*pipto*)" (18:29) like fainting. This poor fellow does not have strength to stand on his feet; he seems hopeless without knowing how or when to pay even 100 denarii. So he merely says: "Have patience with me, and I will pay you" (18:29). In contrast, the first

---

28. Jeremias, Parables, 211, n.13. also, *Jerusalem in the Time of Jesus. An Investigation into Social and Economic Conditions during the New Testament Period* (Philadelphia: Fortress, 1969) 347. See also C. Spicq, *Dieu et l'homme selon le Nouveau Testament* (Paris: Cerf, 1960) 57 n. 5.

slave says, "I will pay you *everything*" (18:26). He hopes that he could pay everything in some day. But this guy who owed him only 100 denarii cannot give him such confident words because of his devastating situation we are not told of. The problem for the first slave is that he does not respond to his fellow with the same mercy; rather, he repeats society's harsh rule on the weak or the marginalized.

The parable continues, and now the friends of this poor slave who owes 100 denarii heard about and saw what had happened between these two and reported to the master. There is no secret in the world, as we read in Mt 10:26: "For there is nothing concealed that will not be disclosed, and nothing secret that will not become known" (also Lk 8:17). This unmerciful or unforgiving servant is put into jailers until he repays full.

In conclusion, all people are debtors. No one can live a life of complete independence from others. Like the seed growing through the conditions of the ground and sun, humans can live because of God's grace. Living in a harsh, unstable world, each needs mercy from others because no one can be safe without it.

This parable of the Unmerciful Servant is well contextualized to fit Matthew's need that all community members are to forgive each other as God already forgave them. In the Christian community, there should not be an everlasting judgment and condemnation of other members. Rather, the community must be on the rise of God's love and forgiveness that will not only solidify the internal bond with one another but attract outsiders because of their superior moral character.

Questions for Reflection/Discussion

1. Think about *han*, a term for minjung theology in Korea. *Han* is a bitter, amassed suffering or pain because of various forms of injustices. Is this poor slave a han-ridden person who cannot pay 100 denarii?

2. Which slave needs mercy, the one who owes 10,000 denarii or the one who owes 100 denarii? The first slave needs adjustment of his debt such as extending due date or installment of the debt payment of time.

3. In what sense is the master like God? In what sense, is he not like God?

Two Sons

> MATTHEW 21:28-31
> 28 "What do you think? A man had two sons; he went to the first and said, 'Son, go and work in the vineyard today.' 29 He answered, 'I will not'; but later he changed his mind and went. 30 The father went to the second and said the same; and he answered, 'I go, sir'; but he did not go. 31 Which of the two did the will of his father?" They said, "The first." Jesus said to them, "Truly I tell you, the tax collectors and the prostitutes are going into the kingdom of God ahead of you."

There are some issues regarding manuscript traditions of verses 29-31.[29] In the Sinaiticus Codex, the first son says no, but later he goes to the field, whereas the second son first says yes, but later he does not go. In the Vatican Codex, the first one says yes but later does not go, whereas the second one says no, but later goes to the field. The New Revised Standard Version (NRSV) and the New International Version (NIV) follow the reading of the Sinaiticus

---

29. There are three kinds of readings in manuscript traditions. Tradition A says that the first son is a good one because he said no, but later repented and went. Tradition B says that the first son is a bad one because he said yes, but did not go. Tradition C is kind of a mixed one in that while the first son said no and repented afterwards, the last son who said no did the father's will. Tradition A (the repenting son comes first) is supported by ℵ C* K W Δ Π, etc. The tradition B (the other son is first in order) is attested by B Θ, etc. The tradition C has the support of D and others. For details, see Bruce Metzger's *Textual Commentary on the Greek New Testament*, 55. See also Davies and Allison, *A Critical and Exegetical Commentary on the Gospel according to S. Matthew* (ICC 26; 3rd ed.; Edinburgh: T. & T. Clark, 1912) 228-29.

Codex. The scholarly consensus is that the Sinaiticus Codex seems close to the original or the early form of the parable. From a textual flow in this parable, a more natural logical reading is that the father asks the first son first and that if he does not say yes, then he will call his second son to ask. The result of two sons' action is embarrassing to the readers because the first one goes to the field after he said no and the second son does not go after saying yes. It is understandable why then the Vatican Codex has a different reading; that is because of the influence of allegorical interpretation in that typically the older brother/son is bad, and the younger son/brother is preferred. This kind of favoritism for the younger brother/son is observed in the Old Testament (Isaac, Jacob, and Joseph). That may have been further influenced by the parable of the father and two sons in Luke 15:21-34 where the older son is allegorically read as Jews while the younger son as a Gentile sinner who repents.

Two sons act differently. The question is: Who followed the will of the father? The answer is the first son, who at first no, but later he changes his mind and goes to the field. But the father is offended by this son because he is disobedient to him. From this son's perspective, if he is unwilling, he must kindly speak to the father about his situation. He could say something like this: "I have things to take care of right now; give me some time and I will see to it." He can make a good conversation with his father. Otherwise, a definitive answer of immediate "no" would be hurtful. Even in later time this first son changes his mind and goes to work. It is never too late. However, the ideal son must be someone who says yes now and goes to work immediately. There is no perfect son in this story. Both sons are not perfect because they did not act immediately according to the father's will.

The second son's response of yes proves to be empty because later he does not go to work. A word without action is dead. Saying yes needs prudence. Matthew 7:21-23 stresses this importance of practice: "Not everyone who says to me, 'Lord, Lord,' will enter the kingdom of heaven, but only the one who does the will of my Father in heaven. On that day many will say to me, 'Lord, Lord, did we not prophesy in your name, and cast out demons in your name, and do many deeds of power in your name?' Then I will declare to them, 'I never knew you; go away from me, you evildoers.'" This scripture is also related to Mt 25:31-46 (the final judgment). Similarly, Mt 7:24-27 talks about doing. Mt 7:24 says: "Everyone then who hears these words of mine and acts on them will be like a wise man who built his house on the rock." The most striking example of this teaching is found in Mt 23:2-3, in which Jesus says to the crowds and his disciples: "The scribes and the Pharisees sit on Moses' seat; therefore, do whatever they teach you and follow it; but do not do as they do, for they do not practice what they teach." At the end of the parable, Jesus says: "Truly I tell you, the tax collectors and the prostitutes are going into the kingdom of God ahead of you" (Mt 29:31). This saying should not be taken as literal; it means that it is easy for these people to accept God's mercy because they are desperate. So they can change their mind and turn to God even at later times. It is never too late.

In conclusion, the parable of the two sons deals with hypocrisy in the community. What is necessary for the community is to live a life of congruence between knowing and acting. A Beautiful word or knowledge alone cannot change the world. The true leader must have this quality that knowing and action must go hand in hand. This parable reminds us of James 2:26: "For just as the body without the spirit is dead, so faith without works is also dead."

Faith in Matthew is an action word. As in the Hebrew Bible faith is never a word of belief only. As we saw the faith of Mary and the Canaanite woman, faith involves courage, trust, and cost. Two sons in this parable represent two kinds of faith: the one that believes something but that does not follow in action; the other that carries out what is mandated even at a later time. Though two sons are dear to the father and will never lose sonship, the honorable son acts on the father's will. The nominal membership in the community or calling of the Lord can make no real change in the kingdom of God.

Matthean Unique Parables

Questions for Reflection/Discussion

1. If you are the father figure in this parable, what do you expect from the two sons?
2. Will the father's relationship with his two sons change after this story?

Great Banquet

MATTHEW 22:1-14 (CF. LUKE 14:16-24; GOS. THOM 64)
1 Once more Jesus spoke to them in parables, saying: 2 "The kingdom of heaven may be compared to a king who gave a wedding banquet for his son. 3 He sent his slaves to call those who had been invited to the wedding banquet, but they would not come. 4 Again he sent other slaves, saying, 'Tell those who have been invited: Look, I have prepared my dinner, my oxen and my fat calves have been slaughtered, and everything is ready; come to the wedding banquet.' 5 But they made light of it and went away, one to his farm, another to his business, 6 while the rest seized his slaves, mistreated them, and killed them. 7 The king was enraged. He sent his troops, destroyed those murderers, and burned their city. 8 Then he said to his slaves, 'The wedding is ready, but those invited were not worthy. 9 Go therefore into the main streets, and invite everyone you find to the wedding banquet.' 10 Those slaves went out into the streets and gathered all whom they found, both good and bad; so the wedding hall was filled with guests. 11 "But when the king came in to see the guests, he noticed a man there who was not wearing a wedding robe, 12 and he said to him, 'Friend, how did you get in here without a wedding robe?' And he was speechless. 13 Then the king said to the attendants, 'Bind him hand and foot, and throw him into the outer darkness, where there will be weeping and gnashing of teeth.' 14 For many are called, but few are chosen."

This parable uses banquet as a source of the story.[30] Perhaps the original simple form of the parable goes like as follows. A certain man planned a great banquet and sent his servants to invite guests. But all of them made various "unreasonable" excuses. Hearing the servants' report, the host asked them to invite anyone on the streets. In a real setting, this hardly happens because to reject invitation means social death. At any rate, in this parable, those who were not invited initially could enter the banquet. This simple parable proper was edited and added by Matthew. In that, the king was raged at the rejection of his invitation and sent troops to kill the murderers of his servants and the city (Jerusalem). However, verses 11-14 are based on Matthew's allegorical interpretation: the king as God, son as Jesus, servants as Jesus's disciples, the invited as Jewish leaders, and the people were taken to the party as all gentiles. Matthew added wedding garment thing, which is not related to the parable proper. In Luke, there is no mention of the king's burning the city. Since he cannot waste what he already prepared, he brought in the poor and the maimed and the lame and the blind (cf. Luke 4:16-30).

From the host's perspective, he at first invited only the powerful people. That was a cultural practice. But later when he received a rejection from them, he extended his invitation to anyone. He must have acted differently initially by inviting those unworthy. But even at a later time, he changed his mind and gave new opportunities to the unworthy. From the unworthy people's perspective, the master's invitation was a total shock because they did not expect. But they were allowed in a great banquet.

This parable has double entendre about its implications for the Matthean community. First, this parable evokes the eschatological wedding banquet where many were invited but ignored the king's invitation. At first, the king (host) invited only the powerful people in society, namely his friends, but they all rejected his hospitality. In a society where a patron-client system was installed, this will not happen because one's refusal to the invitation means a social death. But the king repeatedly sent other slaves. But his

30. Barbara Reid, *Parables for Preachers,* Year A, 180-82.

slaves were mistreated and killed, and his invitation was taken lightly and ignored. So he was enraged and sent his troops to burn the city, which implies Matthew's awareness of the destruction of Jerusalem in 70 CE. Matthew believes that destroying the city (Jerusalem) is itself the punishment of God. This parable reminds the Matthean community of the importance of preparation for the last-day banquet.

Second, this parable also evokes a new community (or the kingdom of God), not based on status or power but based on the unbiased love of God for all. So as his invitation to the powerful was rejected and ignored, the king turns to all others—the good and the bad—because he already prepared a banquet. He asked his slaves to invite *everyone* on the main streets. Now this latter act of the king fits well the Matthean theme: the impartial love of God for all. Both the good and the bad should be included in the second round of the invitation. No one can miss out this important opportunity. However, one difficulty in the parable is how to understand one man's expulsion from the banquet because he wore no wedding robe. Whatever it may mean to the Matthean community, what seems clear is that at a time of the future messianic banquet, there will be a surprise like the reversal in the final judgment scene. So the Matthean community must live up to the kingdom principles as understood by the eschatological community.

Questions for Reflection/Discussion

1. Why did the king (the host) not invite the most unfortunate from the beginning?
2. Which version, Matthew's or Luke's, seems close to the original form of the parable? Why does Matthew tell the story this way?
3. What is the purpose of a banquet? See it from the host's perspective and the invitees' perspective.

Ten Virgins

MATTHEW 25:1-12

1 "Then the kingdom of heaven will be like this. Ten bridesmaids took their lamps and went to meet the bridegroom. 2 Five of them were foolish, and five were wise. 3 When the foolish took their lamps, they took no oil with them; 4 but the wise took flasks of oil with their lamps. 5 As the bridegroom was delayed, all of them became drowsy and slept. 6 But at midnight there was a shout, 'Look! Here is the bridegroom! Come out to meet him.' 7 Then all those bridesmaids got up and trimmed their lamps. 8 The foolish said to the wise, 'Give us some of your oil, for our lamps are going out.' 9 But the wise replied, 'No! there will not be enough for you and for us; you had better go to the dealers and buy some for yourselves.' 10 And while they went to buy it, the bridegroom came, and those who were ready went with him into the wedding banquet; and the door was shut. 11 Later the other bridesmaids came also, saying, 'Lord, lord, open to us.' 12 But he replied, 'Truly I tell you, I do not know you.'

This parable is unique to Matthew and is part of the eschatological discourse (the fifth discourse in Matthew). Matthew stresses the importance of readiness for the end (Wheat and Weed; Budding Fig Tree; Wedding Banquet; Net and Last Judgment). It is questionable this parable comes from Jesus because Jesus is little concerned about the future eschatology. Matthew allegorizes the groom as Jesus (cf. God as a husband in Isa 54:5; Jer 31:31; Hos 2:16).

It is an odd custom that virgins go out to meet the groom.[31] Usually, the relatives or friends of the groom are involved in preparing for the wedding. Wedding culture in Palestine in this time is arranged marriage. Engagement takes place at the bride's house, and the groom pays the dowry with a marriage contract. Then about a year later the official marriage takes place. On the day of the wedding, the groom comes to the bride's house and takes her

---

31. Barbara Reid, *Parables for Preachers*, Year A, 190-99

to his home for the wedding. The groom may come late. Five wise women were mean to other five who did not have enough oil. The oil store must have been closed at that late hour. At any rate, there are two kinds of people: those who prepare and those who do not prepare. That is a Matthean theme we find throughout. Ten virgins all slept when the groom came late. Sleeping or weakness is not a problem. When something happens, there is a big difference between those who are prepared and those not. Those with an oil can act wisely without worries. From Matthew's perspective, this story is about responsibility that cannot be shared.

This parable echoes the parable of a great wedding banquet because it also reminds the Matthean community of the importance of kingdom work now and preparedness for the final messianic banquet. Since ten bridesmaids do not know when the bridegroom will come, they should have prepared lamps with enough oil. Lamps may be compared to the nominal membership as we saw in the parable of two sons earlier. Oil represents the quality work of God. Lamps are needed for lighting, but they would be nothing without oil. So here the "oil" can be, for the community, good works of God, like the first son's action even at a later time in the parable of Two Sons.

Questions for Reflection/Discussion

1. What oils represent in this parable?
2. Can you relate this parable to Matthew 7:24-27 and James 2:26? Read also Matt 5:14-16, Ps 119:105, Prov 13:9.
3. Things can be shared: material, joys, and concerns. But things cannot be shared: service, responsibility, and faith. What do you think?

5

Lukan Unique Parables (I)

Good Samaritan

LUKE 10:30-37

30 Jesus replied, "A man was going down from Jerusalem to Jericho, and fell into the hands of robbers, who stripped him, beat him, and went away, leaving him half dead. 31 Now by chance a priest was going down that road; and when he saw him, he passed by on the other side. 32 So likewise a Levite, when he came to the place and saw him, passed by on the other side. 33 But a Samaritan while traveling came near him; and when he saw him, he was moved with pity. 34 He went to him and bandaged his wounds, having poured oil and wine on them. Then he put him on his own animal, brought him to an inn, and took care of him. 35 The next day he took out two denarii, gave them to the innkeeper, and said, 'Take care of him; and when I come back, I will repay you whatever more you spend.' 36 Which of these three, do you think, was a neighbor to the man who fell into the hands of the robbers?" 37 He said, "The one who showed him mercy." Jesus said to him, "Go and do likewise."

THE PARABLE PROPER IS found in Luke 10:30-37, which extends the conversation between Jesus and the lawyer that started in

LUKAN UNIQUE PARABLES (I)

10:25. The lawyer wants to justify his cause of neighbor theology embedded in his question to Jesus: "Who is my neighbor?" (10:29). To answer this question and teach him about ideal neighbor relations, Jesus tells this parable.

A Jewish man was going down from Jerusalem to Jericho. We are not told about his identity, social class, or work. It is a certain Jewish man who met robbers.[1] According to the Jewish historian Josephus, banditry was widespread and on this road to Jericho, with winter residence, 23 miles south of Jerusalem, with 770 feet below sea level. So anything could happen to anybody in this environment. Now three people pass by one after another. A priest passes by without looking for and taking care of this man. Not all priests can pass by, but this priest passes by. There are no acceptable excuses for him as a priest because he is going down to Jericho away from his priestly duty in Jerusalem. Purity laws are not an issue to him, either, because Jewish laws allow for some exceptions. Priests can bury the abandoned corpse and sometimes, they can look after the sick by touching them. This priest passes by for the unknown reasons, which may not have to with religious or purity concerns. Then the problem falls on the lack of his moral sense or duty. That is a big irony because the priest is the one who must look after this half-dead man. He even does not approach this half-dead man, a fellow Jew. His uncaring act symbolizes his moral death. The love of God (Deut 6:4-9) and the love of neighbor (Lev 19:18) in the Torah are not present with him. Then, similarly, a Levite passes by just like the priest before him. Two of the most religious people do nothing but pass by silently. Now hearers of the parable are also disappointed about this result. Then Jesus introduces a third person, who is an unexpected character, a Samaritan, not a Jew but the object of hatred from the perspective of Jews (2 Kgs 17:24). But he stops at, checks on with, and does everything he could to help the Jewish man in danger. He gives full service and acts in a well-organized manner, taking him on his donkey to the nearby inn and asking the innkeeper to take care of him further

---

1. This parable can be read from the victim's perspective. For that reading, see Robert Funk, "The Good Samaritan as Metaphor," *Semeia* 2(1974) 74-81.

until he comes back. The Samaritan can feel the victim's suffering, defenselessness, and profound vulnerability.[2]

At the end of the story, Jesus asks: "Which of these three, do you think, was a neighbor to the man who fell into the hands of the robbers?" (Lk 10:36). From a traditional Jewish perspective, a neighbor needs help; the one robbed is a neighbor. But Jesus twists the lawyer's original question of "who is my neighbor?" and asks a different question.[3] To this question of Jesus, the lawyer reluctantly answers correctly: "The one who showed him mercy." He never imagines calling the Samaritan neighbor. It is not because the Samaritan is poor and unfortunate but because he is an actor of mercy. Jesus introduces a new idea of neighbor, who is not the object of charity but the subject of God's impartial love for all. The Samaritan is not supposed to help a Jewish man from the perspective of Jews, but he breaks down that cultural boundary. He does everything to help the poor Jewish man and takes full responsibility by taking care of the full process of recovery. The one who helps the needy is a neighbor. This fact raises a great challenge to the lawyer who thinks the neighbor is out there waiting for help. Jesus pushes people to take a role of neighbor themselves. A true neighbor sees the need of a person and takes full responsibility.

The parable of the Good Samaritan lifts the gospel of salvation for the Gentiles by redefining neighbor. Now for the Lukan community, their neighbors are all, especially the marginalized ones. Previously, neighbors were defined by ethnicity or religion. But now neighbors are to be all people. The Lukan community takes the lesson that now they must be neighbors to all in need. The importance of compassion and service to the world is carried out by Luke throughout the narrative. In Luke 4:16-30, Jesus reads the Isaiah scrolls in the local synagogue in his hometown and preaches the importance of God's preferential option for the poor and marginalized. According to Jesus, both Elijah and Elisha

---

2. J. R. Jones, "Love as Perception of Meaning," *Religion and Understanding* (New York MacMillan, 1967), 149-50.

3. Charles Cranfield, "The Good Samaritan," *Theology Today*, 11.3 (1954) 368-372.

were great prophets because they became true neighbors to those in need. They crossed the geographical or psychological borders that foreigners cannot be healed. In the parable of a Rich Man and Lazarus, what is wrong with this rich man is not because he was rich but because he did not extend his hands to the poor man. He became no neighbor to the man in need.

Questions for Reflection/Discussion

1. What will be the best title of this parable?
2. Why do you think this parable is more than about charity?
3. Does Jesus's redefinition of neighbor help to address our problems in the world?

Rich Farmer

Luke 12:16-21
16 Then he told them a parable: "The land of a rich man produced abundantly. 17 And he thought to himself, 'What should I do, for I have no place to store my crops?' 18 Then he said, 'I will do this: I will pull down my barns and build larger ones, and there I will store all my grain and my goods. 19 And I will say to my soul, 'Soul, you have ample goods laid up for many years; relax, eat, drink, be merry.' 20 But God said to him, 'You fool! This very night your life is being demanded of you. And the things you have prepared, whose will they be?' 21 So it is with those who store up treasures for themselves but are not rich toward God."

Thomas 63
Jesus said: There was a rich man who had many possessions. He said: I will use my possessions to sow and reap and plant, to fill my barns with fruit, that I may have

need of nothing. Those were his thoughts in his heart; and in that night he died. He who has ears, let him hear.

The parable of the rich farmer is unique to Luke and found in Luke 12:16-21. This story looks authentic to Jesus since the substance of the story comes from an agricultural setting. Also, there is a motif of reversal between the rich man's happiness and God's calling him a fool. The version in the Gospel of Thomas is a much shorter, simple story than the one in Luke, and it may be the later Gnostic tradition.

The rich farmer repeatedly uses the first person "I" in Luke 12:16-19 and does not think about others in the community. He thinks only about, for, and by himself. So he worries about the space of his warehouses and hatches a new plan: to pull down the current ones and to build much larger ones so he can store all he has and will have in the future. That is a naive dream that can destroy not only his life but the life in the community because his great abundance does not serve the larger community. What must be torn down is not his warehouses to store more crops, but his selfish mind and heart that do not care about other people in his village.[4] The rich man's priority should not be his possessions or crops but his mind and heart geared toward the love of God and the love of neighbor, for which he has to have a sense of a "broken heart" with others. He need not build larger barns because he can store his crops in barns of other people, whose small barns can help him to store all of his crops. Hopefully, he would love to share some crops with them. So the critical issue for him is not simply a lack of charity or a problem of greed but a dull sense of community. He sees only himself; there are no others in his thought and action.

Suddenly, God appears in the story and says to him: "'You fool! This very night your life is being demanded of you. And the things you have prepared, whose will they be?'" (Lk 12:20). The

---

4. The spirituality that the rich man needs is expressed by the prophet Jeremiah: "Circumcise yourselves to the Lord, remove the foreskin of your hearts" (Jer 4:4a). Likewise, Paul says: "Real circumcision is a matter of the heart; it is spiritual and not literal" (Rom 2:29).

rich man is called a fool; this is an irony because he thinks he is very happy because of his abundant crops. He is a fool because he does not know how short his life would be. He does not realize that his very life depends on God and others. He thinks he is self-sufficient, but that is an illusion. No one can be self-reliant. He must have depended on other people in the village because they provided necessary labor to his farm. More than that, without natural conditions and resources such as weather and land he can do nothing. He is also a fool because he believes that his happiness comes from wealth. He sought joy in wrong places. His sense of joy must come from God and others. He can share his crops with others, and then people will respect him. Also, he must learn that joy comes from simple life and contentment. He has to learn how to be content in any circumstance. Like Paul, he must learn what it is to have enough and what it is to have little (Phil 4:11-13). Eventually, what he has to learn is how to be always content. One of the biggest problems in the modern capitalist economy is income disparity. The rich have too much beyond their need and put their wealth in savings accounts or for investment; otherwise, their overflowing resources do not flow to the needy. They put much energy to keep their riches.

This parable of the rich farmer also follows the Lukan theological focus on sharing of wealth for the poor and the community. The rich man's problem is not that he is rich but that he shuts in himself without seeing the need of others. He even does not know how short or vulnerable his life may be. God calls him a fool because he thinks that he can live alone. That is self-deception. So the theology of Luke on the kingdom of God has a focus on the neighborly love that goes beyond the self.

Questions for Reflection/Discussion

1. What is wrong with this rich farmer?
2. What is the main problem he faces?
3. What is the right attitude toward riches?

4. From this story what will be the source of true joy?

Father and Two Sons[5]

LUKE 15:11-32
11 Then Jesus said, "There was a man who had two sons. 12 The younger of them said to his father, 'Father, give me the share of the property that will belong to me.' So he divided his property between them. 13 A few days later the younger son gathered all he had and traveled to a distant country, and there he squandered his property in dissolute living. 14 When he had spent everything, a severe famine took place throughout that country, and he began to be in need. 15 So he went and hired himself out to one of the citizens of that country, who sent him to his fields to feed the pigs. 16 He would gladly have filled himself with the pods that the pigs were eating; and no one gave him anything. 17 But when he came to himself he said, 'How many of my father's hired hands have bread enough and to spare, but here I am dying of hunger! 18 I will get up and go to my father, and I will say to him, "Father, I have sinned against heaven and before you; 19 I am no longer worthy to be called your son; treat me like one of your hired hands."' 20 So he set off and went to his father. But while he was still far off, his father saw him and was filled with compassion; he ran and put his arms around him and kissed him. 21 Then the son said to him, 'Father, I have sinned against heaven and before you; I am no longer worthy to be called your son.' 22 But the father said to his slaves, 'Quickly, bring out a robe— the best one— and put it on him; put a ring on his finger and sandals on his feet. 23 And get the fatted calf and kill it, and let us eat and celebrate; 24 for this son of mine was dead and is alive again; he was lost and is found!' And they began to celebrate. 25 "Now his elder son was in the field; and when he came and approached

---

5. I presented a paper on this parable at the Society of Biblical Literature Annual Meeting in 2014 and this section is a revision of that.

the house, he heard music and dancing. 26 He called one of the slaves and asked what was going on. 27 He replied, 'Your brother has come, and your father has killed the fatted calf, because he has got him back safe and sound.' 28 Then he became angry and refused to go in. His father came out and began to plead with him. 29 But he answered his father, 'Listen! For all these years I have been working like a slave for you, and I have never disobeyed your command; yet you have never given me even a young goat so that I might celebrate with my friends. 30 But when this son of yours came back, who has devoured your property with prostitutes, you killed the fatted calf for him!' 31 Then the father said to him, 'Son, you are always with me, and all that is mine is yours. 32 But we had to celebrate and rejoice, because this brother of yours was dead and has come to life; he was lost and has been found.'"

There is no consensus among scholars about the origin of this parable. Whereas Jack Sanders argues the first part of the parable (vv. 11-24) comes from Jesus and the second part (vv. 25-32) comes through later oral traditions or Luke, Luise Schottroff attributes the entire parable (vv. 11-32) to Lukan origin.[6] But I argue the entire parable comes from Jesus.[7] First, Luke need not create the second part if the original parable did not come with the second part because the first part would be enough to match the two preceding parables of the lost (lost sheep and lost coin). Second, this parable can be well understood in the socio-cultural setting of first-century Palestine under Roman Empire, in which Jesus appears as a countercultural prophet, announces a new rule of God that

---

6. See Jack T. Sanders, "Tradition and Redaction in Lk 15:11-32," *NTS* 15 (1968-69): 433-38; Luise Schottroff, "Das Gleichnis vom verlorenen Sohn," *ZTK* 68 (1971): 27-52; Charles Carlston, "Reminiscence and Redaction in Luke 15:11-32," *JBL* 94.3 (1975): 368-390.

7. Among others, J. Jeremias and Charles Carlston also argue that the entire parable is derived from Jesus. See J. Jeremias, "Zum Gleichnis vom verlorenen Sohn, Luk. 15, 11-32," *TZ* 5 (1949) 228-31; and esp. „Tradition und Redaktion in Lukas 15," *ZNW* 62 (1971) 172-89; Charles Carlston, "Reminiscence and Redaction in Luke 15:11-32," *JBL* 94.3 (1975) 368-390.

challenges a narrow conception of community based on a patron-client system, and offers an alternative vision of a more egalitarian *oikos*. With this historical probability of Jesus's teaching, Jesus uses an irregular, dysfunctional family as a test case to show what is needed in a broken family.

The parable of "the Father and Two Sons" in Luke 15:11-32 is unique to Luke, and its profundity and popularity may be second to none among the parables of Jesus. It has been greatly misunderstood or become controversial because of a long tradition of allegorical interpretation in the older brother/son represents merciless Pharisees or Jews whereas the younger brother/son represents contrite sinners or Gentile Christians forgiven and accepted by the compassionate God.[8] In this allegorical interpretation, the older brother is a symbol of self-righteousness or cold-heartedness whereas the younger brother is a symbol of new creation or humanity in God. This negative reading of the older brother is not new or surprising given the rivalry stories in the Hebrew Bible where Jacob the younger brother is preferred to Esau the older one (Gen 25:19-34).[9] It is so much frequent that in Christian interpretation

---

8. Luke Johnson, *The Gospel of Luke* (Collegeville, MN: Liturgical Press, 1991), 240-42. While Jerome and Augustine connect the older brother with unrepentant Israel, Calvin rejects the Jewish link and connects him with "hypocrites and intolerable pride." For example, Augustine reads the older brother as "the people of Israel following the flesh." See the Letters of St. Jerome, vol. 1, ed. Johannes Quasten and Walter J. Burghardt (Mahwah, NJ: Paulist Press, 1963), 124 (*Letter 21*); Augustine and Calvin are cited in Mikeal Parsons, "The Prodigal's Older Brother: The History and Ethics of Reading Luke 15:25- 32," *Perspectives in Religious Studies* 23 (1996):152, 154. See also Tertullian, *On Repentance* 8.

9. Brandon Scott, *Re-Imagine the World* (Sonoma, CA: Polebridge, 2001), 74-81. In fact, the older brother Esau accepts the younger brother Jacob without conditions when he returns home with fear. Unlike the narrator's comment on Esau, he is the one who is ready to gladly accept his younger brother with mercy. He forgave Jacob already. Seeing Jacob, Esau ran to his brother and kissed him. This scene reminds us of the parable of the Father and Two Sons in Luke 15 that we deal with here. Readers are not told about what happened to Esau to the degree that he changed his mind to accept and welcome his brother without revenge. Obviously, Esau's action resembles the typical mother's. Here we see Esau no longer as the manly hunter-father figure in a traditional family.

LUKAN UNIQUE PARABLES (I)

of this parable or popular culture, the older brother is non-existent.[10] There were "35 extant Prodigal Son plays composed in England before 1642."[11] Shakespeare rarely refers to the older brother and the theme of prodigality is prevalent in his works (*King Lear, Hamlet,* and *the Merchant of Venice* among others).[12] Perhaps his only exception is *the Merchant of Venice* where Shylock is identified with the older brother. But from a communal perspective, all three characters (the father and two sons) are equally important in the family in which the main issue is not who is right or wrong, but how they can live with mercy, justice, and peace. Otherwise, in this parable, there is no motif of sibling preference by the father. Simply, this parable is a family story through which Jesus tells the audience about a new alternative family based on God's rule.[13] The

10. Mikeal Parsons, "The Prodigal's Older Brother: The History and Ethics of Reading Luke 15:25- 32," *Perspectives in Religious Studies* 23 (1996): 147-174.

11. Mikeal Parsons, "The Prodigal's Older Brother: The History and Ethics of Reading Luke 15:25- 32," *Perspectives in Religious Studies* 23 (1996), 155.

12. Ibid., 157.

13. The themes of a parable have to do with Jesus's proclamation of "the good news of God" (*euangelion tou theou*) concerning "the kingdom of God" (*basileia tou theou*). "The good news of God" (*euangelion tou theou*) is God's good news that Jesus brings to the world, and "the kingdom of God" is understood as "God's kingly rule" characterized with mercy, justice, and peace. To manifest the rule of God, Jesus heals the sick, exorcises the possessed people, and teaches his disciples and the crowds through parables, which takes one third of his teaching in the synoptic tradition. According to J. D. Crossan, there are three kinds of parables of Jesus that focus on God's rule: (1) "parables of advent"; (2) "parables of reversal"; (3) "parables of action." J. D. Crossan, *In Parables: The Challenge of the Historical Jesus* (Sonoma, CA: Polebridge, 1992), 36. The parable of "the father and two sons" in Luke 15:11-32 addresses all of these three aspects of God's rule in the world. First, regarding the advent of God's rule, this parable introduces a new radical egalitarian community where all are embraced without conditions. This community of God is radically different from the typical communities in the Roman Empire run by the patron-client system. Second, regarding the reversal of God's rule, because of the radical advent of God's rule in the here and now, the current system or thought is challenged and reversed in ways that God's rule may be reestablished. In fact, the father in this parable does not follow society's norm that has to maintain a clear boundary between father and children and between reward and punishment. Third, regarding the action of God's rule, the parable exhorts the readers to act based on the new vision of a family, seeking an ultimate

The Parable in the Lukan Context

first-century Mediterranean society was a communal, dyadic culture where one could not live in isolation.

To unpack the parable of "the father and two sons" in Luke we need careful examination of all three "lost" parables (the lost sheep, the lost coin, and the lost son) in Luke 15. Note that Luke 15:1-2 is placed before the parable begins: "Now all the tax collectors and sinners were coming near to listen to him. And the Pharisees and the scribes were grumbling and saying, 'This fellow welcomes sinners and eats with them.'" This text foregrounds the importance of inclusivism of gentile sinners. So in the first two "lost" parables, Luke emphasizes the themes of repentance and forgiveness: "Just so, I tell you, there will be more joy in heaven over one sinner who repents than over ninety-nine righteous persons who need no repentance" (15:7; 15:10).[14] But these parables told by Jesus have nothing to do with such themes of repentance or forgiveness since the lost sheep or the lost coin cannot return or repent.[15] Rather, these parables are about the owners who have lost and searched for the lost at all cost. But for the third parable of "the father and two sons" (Luke 15:11-32), the issue is more complex than in the first two. First, unlike the first two parables, there is no clear Lukan redaction within this parable, which implies that Luke finds it interesting on its own. This is perhaps because of the younger son/brother's "conniving" gesture of regretting and his return, which could be read as genuine repentance.[16] Second, unlike the first two parables, this parable does not end with "feasting and rejoicing" at the party, and the story continues with tensions among the family members.[17] There is no sign the two brothers will be reconciled

---

reconciliation of a community.

14. In the Matthean version of the lost sheep (Matt 18:12-14) there is no statement about repentance for the sinner.

15. Amy Jill Levine, *Short Stories by Jesus*, 27.

16. Amy Jill Levine, *Short Stories by Jesus*, 53.

17. Ibid., 45-6.

eventually. Obviously, the father is happy about his newly found son, and yet he has to make sure that his sons are reconciled with each other. Third, whereas the first two "lost" parables deal with the care for lost sheep and the lost coin, the third "lost" parable has more to do with family or community where all members should play a certain role to achieve union or reconciliation. The father cares for both sons, unlike the *paterfamilias* who runs with authority or matriarchs in the Hebrew Bible who favor the younger son (Gen 25:19-34).

With the above understanding about the third "lost" parable in Luke, the Lukan point is that God's rule is not exclusive to a particular group of people. It is open to all. The father in the parable affirms the place of the older brother and what the father wants is the holistic community once again. Given this parable's open-ended character, the Lukan community seeks a more open community. The condition for joining such a new inclusive community is repentance. But in the parable proper, the younger son/brother does not repent from his heart other than trying to avoid such dire misery; it would be hardly the case this parable emphasizes the importance of repentance and forgiveness. Rather, regardless of his repentance, the father is ready to accept him with mercy. The Lukan inclusive gospel fits well in the Lukan audience—"a group of late-first century churches of diverse social composition" where all are welcomed with a new vision of God's *oikos*.[18] Especially given the Lukan theology of the universal gospel for all people beyond the Jewish boundary, the importance of unity in diversity in a newly emerging Christian community cannot be overemphasized. With a new vision of an alternative community based on God's mercy, justice, and peace, Lukan audience must support each other, seeking a holistic, livable community for all.

---

18. Robert Tannehill, *Luke* (Nashville, TN: Abingdon Press, 1996), 24.

Dysfunctional Family Story with Struggles

Mediterranean society is a culture of kinship whose domain covers "a broad range of institutions: genealogy and descent, marriage and divorce, and dowry systems and inheritance."[19] Kinship in the ancient Mediterranean society impacts every part of life and every other social domain. In this kin-world context we have to read the parable of Jesus by locating his parabolic message in the family as Levine notes in her most recent book:[20]

> In its original context, the parable of the Prodigal Son would not have been heard as a story of repentance or forgiveness, a story of works-righteousness and grace, or a story of Jewish xenophobia and Christian universalism. Instead, the parable's messages of finding the lost, of reclaiming children, of reassessing *the meaning of family* offer not only good news, but better news (italics are mine for emphasis).

With the reading lens of family, we may think of several aspects of family dynamics. First, the parable of "the father and two sons" is a story of a dysfunctional family that needs resolution and reconciliation.[21] The family loses its equilibrium and stability because of the younger son's immature, rash action. The younger son dishonors his father by asking for a share of his property (15:12), which is shameful to his father. In Jewish tradition, inheritance is not transferred until the parents die to prevent their children from fighting with each other or from stopping to honor them (Num 36:7-9; 27:8-11; Sirach 33:20-24).[22]

---

19. K. C. Hanson, "Kinship," *BTB* 24 (1994): 183-94. See also Jerome Neyrey, "First-Century Personality," in Jerome Neyrey, ed. *The Social World of Luke-Acts: Models for Interpretation* (Peabody, MA: Hendrickson Publishers, 1991), 67-96.

20. Amy Jill Levine, *Short Stories by Jesus: The Enigmatic Parables of a Controversial Rabbi* (New York, NY: HarperOne, 2014), 28.

21. Ibid., 62.

22. A similar piece of advice is in the *Babylonian Talmud*, Baba Mezia, 75B: "He who transfers his property to his children in his lifetime" is someone that needs to be shunned.

Second, this parable deals with the role of the father (or a parent) in the family, who is unlike the *paterfamilias* in society.[23] The father behaves unconventionally and risks his honor as a typical father in a village. He is doubly shamed since he fails "to discipline his son ... by agreeing to his son's dishonorable request."[24] Besides, this father is mother-like and has a weak image throughout the story, as he waits for his son outside of his house and hugs and kisses him upon his return. Brandon Scott notes the father's mother-like image: "The father combines in himself the maternal and paternal roles. As a father, he is a failure, but as a mother, he is a success."[25] The father is also very much overreacting to the younger son's return home and prepares a big banquet and invites all village people. Being overjoyed, the father could forget about his older son, but he seeks him out and explains why he does so. To our surprise, there is no mother or daughters in this parable. However irregular the family may be, the father's role in the family is non-conventional yet enlightening. The father waits outside of his house and sees his son from afar and runs to meet him. Immediately, the father asks the servants to prepare a big banquet to welcome his son. This father also is equally concerned with the older son, calling him "child" (*teknon*) and assuring him that "all that is mine is yours" (15:31). At the same time the father explains why he throws a lavish feast to his younger son: "For this *your brother* was dead, and is alive; he was lost, and is found" (15:32).

---

23. I do not think that the older son/brother resembles the imperial system of the Roman Empire whereas the father is considered a model of challenge to the system. For example, Rohun Park elevates the father's countercultural role against the Empire represented by the older son. But such a view misses the aspects of family story where the goal is not who is right but to get ultimate peace and justice. See Rohun Park, "Revisiting the parable of the prodigal son for decolonization: Luke's reconfiguration of *oikos* in Luke 15:11-32," *Biblical Interpretation* 17 (2009): 507-520.

24. See Amy Jill Levine, *Short Stories by Jesus*, 50.

25. See Brandon Scott, *Hear Then the Parable* (Minneapolis, MN: Fortress, 1990), 122. See also his work *Re-Imagine the World* (Sonoma, CA: Polebridge, 2001), 82. See also Alicia Batten, "Dishonor, Gender and the Parable of the Prodigal Son," *Toronto Journal of Theology* 13 (1997): 187-200.

From this, it is clear the father cares for both of his sons.[26] Note how the father's language reflects his older son's condescending attitude toward his brother: "this son of yours..." (Lk 15:30). Therefore, this parable follows no system of reward and punishment in which the bad are punished, and the good are rewarded. From the perspective of traditional Jewish theology, the father should not act like the one in the parable. He has to scold and punish him and then he can restore him to the family. The father's unconditional acceptance based on his mercy is exceptional and may cause the state of antinomianism. According to the patron-client system or the honor-shame culture, the father should not act like the way he does in the parable. However, the challenge is this mother-like father becomes an alternative model of a family or community that follows God's rule—characterized by mercy and justice.[27]

Third, this parable deals with a matter of justice in the family. When the older brother/son hears news about his brother's return and the father's extravagant banquet for his brother, he is angry and refuses to enter his father's house. He complains to his

---

26. This parable also does not follow the traditional storyline of sibling rivalries in the Hebrew Bible where matriarchs are involved in favoring the younger brother over against the older brother (for example: Cain and Abel, Ishmael and Isaac, Esau and Jacob, and Judah and his brothers and Joseph). Perhaps it is not accidental in this parable that the mother does not appear because of that association with biblical matriarchs. A typical expression about sibling rivalry is found in Malachi 1:2-3: "I have loved you, says the Lord. But you say, 'How have you loved us?' Is not Esau Jacob's brother? says the Lord. Yet I have loved Jacob but I have hated Esau; I have made his hill country a desolation and his heritage a desert for jackals." In such sibling tales, we find the logic of "either/or": if one is chosen, the other is a loser. This kind of sibling favoritism with a younger son/brother appears in the Jewish *midrash* of Psalms 9, where the king loves the little son more than the grown-ups. The movie *Amadeus* (1984) may be a modern reincarnation of this tale of rivalry favoritism: Moses representing a profligate talented young man and the older Antonio Salieri as less talented. But this parable does not endorse such logic. Rather, the father cares for both sons. The older son is guaranteed to receive the inheritance while the younger son is welcomed back to the home. Although complete peace and justice is yet to be seen since this parable is open-ended, one thing is clear: the father shows no partiality to either of his sons.

27. See Alicia Batten, "Dishonor, Gender and the Parable of the Prodigal Son," *Toronto Journal of Theology* 13 (1997): 187-200.

father because life is unfair to him. From a perspective of a family in the first century, the older brother/son is a good man, diligent for the family.[28] His complaints should not be taken so negatively or narrow-mindedly that he may be a cold-hearted man. He is a good son who raises issues of justice. Similarly, his concerns are legitimate because he cares about the well-being of the whole family. His role of prosecutor seems a good and necessary job for the healthy family. Otherwise, his point is not to ruin his younger brother or to disobey his father. He has a right to speak up in the family by his sound thought and judgment. He is thoughtful and patient enough not to rush to his brother. He could have run to his brother and smashed him by his cheek. Rather, he stays outside the house and takes the time to digest and go through this unusual experience. This parable as a family story leaves us with the unresolved questions: Is the younger brother/son accepted unconditionally or is he accepted because he repented? Is the father's overreaction to his son necessary? Is the older brother/son's voice of justice legitimate? How can the justice in the family be restored? For eventual reconciliation between these family members what should be done in the process?

Toward Reconciliation

The meaning of this parable is decided not solely by Jesus in his time or Luke in his time, but by the flesh-and-blood reader who not only hears what the text says but also interacts with it given

28. The older son's slave language in Luke 15:29-30 may not mean his relationship with the father but his hard work for the father as son. See LaHurd, Carol Schersten LaHurd, "Re-viewing Luke 15 with Arab Christian Women," in Amy-Jill Levine, ed. *A Feminist Companion to Luke* (London; New York: Sheffield Academic, 2002), 246-268 (264). Regarding the positive light of the old brother, see Donald Juel, "The Strange Silence of the Bible," *Interpretation* 51 (1997): 5-19; Nancy Duff, "Luke 15:11-32," *Interpretation* 49 (1995): 66-69; Heikki Räisänen, "The Prodigal Gentile and His Jewish Christian Brother, Luke 15:11-32," in F. Van Segbroek *et al.* eds. *The Four Gospels* (Leuven: Leuven University Press, 1992), 1617-36; Charles Carlston, "Reminiscence and Redaction in Luke 15:11-32," *JBL* 94 (1975): 368-90. See also O'Rourke, "Some Notes on Luke 15:11-32," *NTS* 18 (1972):431-433.

his or her perspective. Meaning or interpretation of biblical texts involves "the intersection of text, context, and hermeneutics."[29] In such a frame of critical interpretation, a parable is an ideal place we can engage because it invites us to think deeply and find answers for ourselves.[30] Since the parable is open-ended, we wonder about the end of the story. If there is an ideal scenario of the end of the story, what is it and how can it be achieved? There are many unresolved questions that await the reader's engagement: whether the brothers will have time to talk with each other? What should the father do more than he did already? Since the real peace and justice is yet to be seen with this family, what will be the next step that each member must work out healing and ultimate reconciliation?

---

29. Yung Suk Kim, *Christ's Body in Corinth: The Politics of a Metaphor* (Minneapolis, MN: Fortress, 2008), 8.

30. C.H. Dodd's definition of the parable is pertinent to this essay: "At its simplest the parable is a metaphor or simile drawn from nature or common life, arresting the hearer by its vividness or strangeness, and leaving the mind in sufficient doubt about its precise application to tease it into active thought." See C. H. Dodd, *The Parable of the Kingdom* (New York: Charles Scribner's Sons, 1961), 5. Similarly, according to Marcus Borg, "a parable is a story cast alongside of life for the sake of leading the audience to see something differently." See Marcus Borg, *Jesus: The Life, Teaching, and Relevance of a Religious Revolutionary* (New York: HaperCollins, 2008), 259. Both Dodd and Borg emphasize that a parable must engage the reader. For example, if the kingdom of God is compared to leaven hidden in three measures of flour (Matt 13:33; Luke 13:20-21), the reader has to wonder in what sense the kingdom of God is associated with the leaven. At first hand it is not easy to understand the link between them because leaven usually symbolizes corruption or defilement in the New Testament (Matt 16:5-12; Mark 8:15; Luke 12:1-12; Gal 5:9; 1 Cor 5:1-8). But Jesus uses it positively in this parable. In it, Jesus challenges the reader to see the hidden power or role of the leaven taken and hidden by a woman, not by a man or an elite person. Jesus perhaps thinks of the leaven as a metaphor that represents social outcasts who are considered nobodies in society and yet who can do great works in God's kingdom. See Brandon Scott, *Re-Imagine the World*, 24-34. The bottom line is that a parable is not an exemplary story or moral lesson but a story that invokes the reader to re-imagine the world and God's rule that needs small people or nobodies. As a result, the reader may change his or her views about God's kingdom and act differently because of this parable's challenge about the re-imagined world.

LUKAN UNIQUE PARABLES (I)

A Path Toward Reconciliation

The groundwork for possible reconciliation is already paved by the father who shows mercy unconditionally, and yet there should be more work done by all members of the family. Therefore, we need to examine briefly what each member must do for eventual reconciliations. First, the father is overjoyed by his son's return, and because of that, he does not listen to him. He does not speak to his son, either. He has to continue to listen to his older son's request of justice, which must be met somehow in the family. The father is not a perfect father. Second, the younger son must begin his full confession story after he is welcomed. It seems the son did not repent; instead, he may have uttered "the empty words Pharaoh mouths to stop the plagues."[31] Exodus 10:16 reads, "Pharaoh hurriedly summoned Moses and Aaron and said, 'I have sinned against the LORD your God, and against you.'" Perhaps this poor son fixes his eyes only on food to get out of this dire condition of life or death. In doing so, he prepares this prayer. Upon arrival at home, he omits a part he prepared as in 15:19: "Treat me like one of your hired hands."[32] Given his dire situation of life or death, his focus is rather on food and his "granted" place in the father's house. Perhaps he thought he did not have to say more because of the father's overreaction. Regardless of his purpose about repentance, one thing he did well is he returned home. After his return home, there is a long way he must prove that he changes his mind with good deeds. He also needs to say to his older brother he did wrong in the past. Third, the older brother also must approach his brother and listen to him. He can also share why he felt bad about his brother. He also can talk about his work experience in the field under the scorching sun for the family. He also has to continue to talk with his father about the meaning of his brother's return and related issues of justice and peace. Fourth all the family members must sit at the same table, sharing bread and wine with each other, savoring both sour and sweet moments of life. True relationship

---

31. Amy Jill Levine, *Short Stories by Jesus*, 53.
32. Robert Tannehill, *Luke*, 241.

or reconciliation is neither a one-way channel nor a blind or naïve love without a mutual understanding. There must be both individual and communal efforts for mutual understanding and solidarity. Each person's pain or wounds must be recognized, discussed, and healed: the father's pain of losing the younger one; the older brother's pain that justice is not served; and the younger brother's pain he lost all.

In the parable, as we saw before, the most important foundation and starting point toward reconciliation are the father's unconditional and impartial mercy and trust set long before the younger son's return. Although *paterfamilias* in society considers the father in this parable a fool who sacrifices his honor and mismanages his family, the father acts against the system of reward and punishment. Justice and peace must follow mercy.

We have interpreted this parable from the perspective of a family in which no one is excluded. This father figure in the parable is concerned about the whole family where the question of who is right is not important. What eventually matters to him is how to heal and unite his family. The first thing to do is to accept the immature son without conditions. So mercy is the first thing; and eventually, justice should follow as time goes by.

We have read this parable given the dysfunctional family story where the goal is reconciliation, which needs time and right order. Mercy/love is the first thing that is necessary to the crisis. Justice must follow as time goes by. Reconciliation is not reached once and for all. There must be a continual work in the cycle: from mercy to justice to peace.

Questions for Reflection/Discussion

1. Who is the main character in this parable? What will be the best title of this parable?

2. Do you believe the entire parable of Luke 15:11-32 comes from Jesus? What is Jesus's primary challenging point in this story?

3. Do you believe that sibling rivalry is a key issue in this parable, or something else?
4. How is the father in this parable described?
5. For possible future reconciliation in this dysfunctional family, what more work is necessary?

6

Lukan Unique Parables (II)

Unjust Steward

LUKE 16:1-8A

1 Then Jesus said to the disciples, "There was a rich man who had a manager, and charges were brought to him that this man was squandering his property. 2 So he summoned him and said to him, 'What is this that I hear about you? Give me an accounting of your management, because you cannot be my manager any longer.' 3 Then the manager said to himself, 'What will I do, now that my master is taking the position away from me? I am not strong enough to dig, and I am ashamed to beg. 4 I have decided what to do so that, when I am dismissed as manager, people may welcome me into their homes.' 5 So, summoning his master's debtors one by one, he asked the first, 'How much do you owe my master?' 6 He answered, 'A hundred jugs of olive oil.' He said to him, 'Take your bill, sit down quickly, and make it fifty.' 7 Then he asked another, 'And how much do you owe?' He replied, 'A hundred containers of wheat.' He said to him, 'Take your bill and make it eighty.' 8 And his master commended the unjust manager because he had acted shrewdly; *for the children of this age are more shrewd in dealing with their own generation than are the children*

Lukan Unique Parables (II)

of light. 9 And I tell you, make friends for yourselves by means of dishonest wealth so that when it is gone, they may welcome you into the eternal homes. 10 "Whoever is faithful in a very little is faithful also in much; and whoever is dishonest in a very little is dishonest also in much. 11 If then you have not been faithful with the dishonest wealth, who will entrust to you the true riches? 12 And if you have not been faithful with what belongs to another, who will give you what is your own? 13 No slave can serve two masters; for a slave will either hate the one and love the other, or be devoted to the one and despise the other. You cannot serve God and wealth."

LUKE 16:1-8A MAY BE the parable proper and 16: 8b-13 are the Lukan redaction because it reflects Lukan theology such as the right use of money. Otherwise, Luke does not question the source of wealth. This parable is unique to Luke, and the steward is about to lose his job because the charge is made against him he wasted the master's money. Then, he acts shrewdly to protect not only his job but the others in a community by reducing their debt. This parable does not give us full information about what is going on here. We are not told about how the steward squandered the master's property. The steward is charged with wasting of his master's property, which means his master's credit and all his hard work. But the steward practiced usury because he is called "unjust" by his master. The problem is not his dishonesty to his master but his wrongdoing about the property of his master. In verse 8, *oikonomon tes adikias* can be better translated as "the unjust steward." The master's honor was severely damaged.[1]

On hearing the news of his imminent dismissal, the steward struggles and realizes that he made a big mistake and that he ruined not only the reputation of his master but also other people's lives. So he corrects his wrongdoing so he may be accepted into the community later when fired. He calls the debtors and reduces the debt by a significant amount. He may have considered each debtor's situation and reduced the debt according to their ability

---

1. David Landry and Ben May, "Honor Restored: New Light on the Parable of the Prudent Steward (Luke 16:1-8a)," 287-309.

to repay. All he wants is to buy good relationship from the debtors. He not only cleans up all wrongdoings (such as high-interest rate) but reduces the debt to the proper affordable size so they can afford to pay. The result is the master commends his manager's work as shrewd. We can hardly think the master praises his selfish, smart tactic to survive. The master points out the steward's wise act (*phronomos*) that corrects his wrongdoing and restores his master's credit.[2] Because his corruption and wrongdoing have been cleaned up, now the master's money can come back smoothly to him. The master's reputation is also recovered because of that cleanness. So economically speaking, his property will be handled well than before. Because of this rectification by the manager, people in the village will find themselves stronger than before. The business environment is stable and healthy. Perhaps the master also commends his manager for taking care of the community. This guy changes his lifestyle, based on relationships with people in the community. He saves himself by saving others. His master is also content with him. This parable teaches about what is most important in the community life; it is not the money or the power but the solid relationships through which people help each other. In the complexly-entangled creditor-debtor relationships, people are often treated as a commodity, and money takes humanity down. From the steward's act, we learn that it is never too late that people can change their life in times of crises.

This parable can be understood in line with other parables that underline the importance of helping the need: The Good Samaritan, the Rich Farmer, and the Rich Man and Lazarus. The point of the parable for the Lukan community is that the kingdom of God cannot become a reality to him/her unless he/she takes care of others in need. The loan manager did the wrong things but later realized that he could not survive if he continued to practice usury. He was smart enough not only because of his tactics to survive but because of his helping others in debt by reducing it significantly. The master praised such an act of his smartness. Otherwise, the

---

2. William Herzog has a different view that the master here is an abusive rich person, and his steward is challenging such a malpractice of wealth.

manager is not commended by his master because of his dishonest use of money. Luke then added more verses to this parable proper (16:8b-13); the added material is complex and often loses its connection with the early part (16:1-8a), which is the original part of Jesus's parable. In 16:8b-13, some common themes are connected with the parable proper: good use of wealth and making friends. A smart person serves God with wealth. When people say they love God, they also have to show their love by making friends with wealth. A typical behavioral pattern in Luke is that people serve wealth only. That is why they are told not to serve two masters together; while serving wealth only, they cannot say they love God. So the real smart person in the kingdom of God will serve God with wealth. So in a strict sense, the choice is not between God and money, as if money were evil, but between God with wealth and wealth without God. From the overall Lukan theology, what is required is to share power and wealth with others.

Questions for Reflection/Discussion

1. Why do you think the master praises his steward's act as shrewd?
2. Why does the steward change his mind in this parable? What makes him change?
3. Why is debt cut important in this parable?

Rich Man and Lazarus

LUKE 16:19-31
19 "There was a rich man who was dressed in purple and fine linen and who feasted sumptuously every day. 20 And at his gate lay a poor man named Lazarus, covered with sores, 21 who longed to satisfy his hunger with what fell from the rich man's table; even the dogs would come and lick his sores. 22 The poor man died and was carried away by the angels to be with Abraham. The rich

man also died and was buried. 23 In Hades, where he was being tormented, he looked up and saw Abraham far away with Lazarus by his side. 24 He called out, 'Father Abraham, have mercy on me, and send Lazarus to dip the tip of his finger in water and cool my tongue; for I am in agony in these flames.' 25 But Abraham said, 'Child, remember that during your lifetime you received your good things, and Lazarus in like manner evil things; but now he is comforted here, and you are in agony. 26 Besides all this, between you and us a great chasm has been fixed, so that those who might want to pass from here to you cannot do so, and no one can cross from there to us.' 27 He said, 'Then, father, I beg you to send him to my father's house— 28 for I have five brothers— that he may warn them, so that they will not also come into this place of torment.' 29 Abraham replied, 'They have Moses and the prophets; they should listen to them.' 30 He said, 'No, father Abraham; but if someone goes to them from the dead, they will repent.' 31 He said to him, 'If they do not listen to Moses and the prophets, neither will they be convinced even if someone rises from the dead.'"

Scholars dispute whether the entire text of 16:19-31 is from Jesus.[3] Possibly, 16:27-31 is a Lukan creation. But the entire text derives from Jesus because there is a motif of reversal which is a common technique in storytelling. There is a reversal of the fate of the rich man and Lazarus.

The parable of the Rich Man and Lazarus is unique to Luke. Whereas Lazarus is comforted and resting in the bosom of Abraham, the rich man is being tormented in Hades. Lazarus is there with Abraham because he is the son of Abraham; otherwise, he did not earn his place by good deeds. The rich man is in Hades because he, explicitly or implicitly, ignored Lazarus and did not stretch his hands to him. This implies that who is living next to a person is an important ethical consideration.[4]

---

3. Robert Funk, *The Parables of Jesus: Red Letter Edition* (Sonoma, CA: 1988), 64.

4. George Knight, "Luke 16:19-31: The Rich Man and Lazarus," *Review and Expositor*, 94.2 (1997) 277-283.

The parable does not give us full information about the rich man and Lazarus. In verses 19-21, the rich man and Lazarus are contrasted; whereas the former has many friends and invites them to his sumptuous party, Lazarus has no friends and waits for mercy outside the rich man's house. This rich man considers his rich as blessings of God and is too busy enjoying such blessings with his friends to see Lazarus, sitting and begging at the gate of his house. Fine linen and purple are paired to indicate kings who often wear the best attire (Prov 31:22; Jos., Ant. 3.154; Rev 18:12; Esth 1:6) and purple dress (Judg 8:26; Esth 8:15). His name is unknown. That is an irony. The poor man is Lazarus, so "God has helped." He is a poor (*ptochos*) man, which differs from a beggar (*prosaites*)! While beggar actively begs (Mk 10:46; John 9:8), Lazarus is a poor man, who was at the gate of the rich man. We are not told how he ended up there. We can think of possible reasons such as economic exploitation by the elite. So he eats scraps and competes with the hungry street dogs that lick at his sores. No scene can be more disastrous than this.

In verses 22-26, there are three persons appearing: Abraham, Lazarus, and the rich man (still unnamed). Two men's fate is reversed, but this time, Lazarus is in the bosom (*kolpos*) of Abraham, which is a symbolic place of honor. We are reminded that Jacob, Aaron, and Moses "was gathered to his fathers" upon their death (Gen 49:33; Num 27:13; Deut 32:50). To the same place of honor, Lazarus is placed. That is a big surprise since he does not earn it by his work. The only reason is that he is also a child of Abraham. The rich man is being tormented in Hades, the netherworld, (Lk 10:15; Acts 2:27). The Greek Hades is equivalent to Sheol in Hebrew, which is not a place of punishment but a place of darkness (Isa 14:9; Job 26:5-6; Ps 6:6), which is reserved for the wicked (1 Enoch 22:3-13).

Now the rich man appeals to Abraham, calling him "Father Abraham." This rich man appeals to his sonship to Abraham. But he does not know John Baptist's teaching: "Bear fruits worthy of repentance. Do not begin to say to yourselves, 'We have Abraham as our ancestor'; for I tell you, God is able from these stones to raise up children to Abraham (Lk 3:8; cf. John 8:39). Abraham calls this rich man "my child," but he says he cannot do anything for him now because it is too late for him to do anything. The rich man's time and life are done now. Nothing he can do to send him back to the world. What he did in the world leads him to what he is now.

Verses 27-31 are an added text by the evangelist, but I believe they are part of the original parable. In it, the rich man still does not see Lazarus as his brother and treats him as his servant. So he asks Abraham to send Lazarus as his messenger to his brothers on earth. He does not say sorry to Lazarus. He is so focused on himself. But Abraham rejects his request because there are already prophets to whom they can listen.

In conclusion, this story serves practical purposes: Do not ignore the poor and do something now before too late. Justice will be done somehow even after this life. Again, all of these should be taken as an ethical mandate.[5] This parable also reminds us of Jesus's saying in Luke 18:25 (also, Mt 19:24 and Mk 10:25): "Indeed, it is easier for a camel to go through the eye of a needle than for someone who is rich to enter the kingdom of God." Here the kingdom of God is not a place or time but God's rule. In Jesus's time, the rich are busy keeping their rich and do not have concerns with the poor or the marginalized. In John 3:3 also, Jesus talks about God's rule: "Very truly, I tell you, no one can see the kingdom of God without being born from above." "Being born from above" is a metaphor that refers to those who live by the Spirit of truth. Those who are born from the Spirit seek God's will or God's rule in the here and now.

As we have seen before, the Lukan theological focus is very consistent regarding the new concept of neighbor (for example in the parable of the Good Samaritan) and the need of helping others regardless of their conditions. This parable of the Rich Man and Lazarus is most outstanding regarding the sharing community of

---

5. Justice of God will be implemented eventually after it is not realized in the present. This idea is called "theodicy" in that God is justified. This idea of theodicy is found for example in Dan 12:2, 1 Enoch 22:8-11, and 2 Esdr 7:36-37.

love. What is wrong with this rich man is because he became no neighbor to Lazarus. He had a sumptuous dinner every day with his good friends to whom Lazarus does not belong. In Lukan theology on the kingdom of God, the poor and the marginalized are to be helped out not simply because they are destitute but because they are also the children of God.

Questions for Reflection/Discussion

1. What is wrong with this rich man? What is the main problem he faces? If he was a good man to his friends and became rich by his hard work, was he still responsible for this poor man sitting at his gate?
2. What may have happened to Lazarus before his ending up with begging?
3. What is the basis of Abraham's welcoming of Lazarus?
4. Can you relate the importance of "today" to this parable, which is an important theme of Luke (2:11; 4:21; 5:26; 19:5; 23:43)?

Unjust Judge and Widow

LUKE 18:1-8

18:1 Then Jesus told them a parable about their need to pray always and not to lose heart. 2 He said, "In a certain city there was a judge who neither feared God nor had respect for people. 3 In that city there was a widow who kept coming to him and saying, 'Avenge (ekdikeo) me justice against my opponent.' 4 For a while he refused; but later he said to himself, 'Though I have no fear of God and no respect for anyone, 5 yet because this widow keeps bothering me, I will grant her justice, so that she may not wear me out by continually coming.'" 6 And the Lord said, "Listen to what the unjust judge says. 7 And

> *will not God grant justice to his chosen ones who cry to him day and night? Will he delay long in helping them? 8 I tell you, he will quickly grant justice to them. And yet, when the Son of Man comes, will he find faith on earth?"* (Italics indicate the Lukan addition to the parable proper).

The original part of the parable includes 18:2-5, and the rest (18:1, 6-8) is the Lukan addition that stresses the importance of prayer —one of the important themes in Luke.[6] In Luke, Jesus prays regularly, and at critical turning points: at his baptism (3:21); before his choice of the Twelve (6:12); before Peter's declaration of Jesus as the Messiah (9:18); at the Transfiguration (9:28-29); before his arrest on the Mount of Olives (22:39-46); and on the cross (23:46). Verses 6-8 is a Luke's comment as we see from the fact that "the Lord" is out of step with the narrative flow.

In ancient Israel and first century CE in Palestine, the most vulnerable in society include widows, orphans, and foreigners. This parable emphasizes the importance of justice for the marginalized. Widows are a symbol of the marginalized and the weak in society who cannot live without the mercy of others, but the widow in this parable does not sit and wait for justice. She is persistent until her justice is granted. While Luke uses this parable to stress the importance of prayer, the parable proper is about justice.

In this parable, the judge is atypical and does not care for the marginalized. He is a bad character. The main character is the widow and the focus is on her persistence seeking justice amid an unjust world. God's rule of justice is not coming without activation fee, which is the widow's bold and persistent faith. Her prayerful, justice-driven action, not mere prayer, is the key to reading this parable.

The image of the judge here greatly differs from the biblical tradition where judges have the fear of God and respect for people (2 Chr 19:6-7). Psalm 111:10 reads: "The fear of the Lord

---

6. Luke emphasizes various examples of prayer and figures: Mary (1:46-55), Simeon (2:29-32), Anna (2:38), Jesus (10:21-22) praying in thanksgiving. Prayers of praise by Zacchaeus (1:67-79), the heavenly host (2:13-14) and shepherds (2:20), disciples' intercessory prayer (11:1-4), prayer for their enemies, Jesus prayer for forgiveness for those who crucify him (23:34).

is the beginning of wisdom" (cf. Prov 1:7; also Lev 19:14, 32). This judge is uncaring and unmoved by the widow's persistent request for justice. The irony is that while he does not fear God, he fears this woman because she keeps coming and bothering him. In v. 5, the verb *hypopiazein* implies such a bothering pressure to him since the term is a boxing term (for example 1 Cor 9:26-27), which means "to strike under the eye."

The widow is unconventional like a Canaanite woman in Matt 15:21-28. Usually, the widow is the most vulnerable and needs special attention from community (Exod 22:22; Deut 10:18; 27:19; Isa 1:17; 10:2; Jer 22:3; Ps 94:6; 146:9; Ezek 22:7; 44:22; Zech 7:9-10; Mal 3:5). They are voiceless and weak. However, the widow in this parable is unlike that of the tradition. She boldly faces the impervious judge, voicing her demand until heard. While we are not told about her specific unjust situation, the obvious thing is that she has an issue that must be heard. So she kept coming. What the widow wants is "avenge her." The verb *ekdikeo* in 18:3 is to avenge. What she wants is justice.

In conclusion, the judge here is not to be confused with God. According to the Lukan interpretation of this parable proper, the judge must be God, who hears his people. This judge is unlike God. The point of the parable is the widow's faith and action for justice. Her persistent faith requires a cost, courage, and patience. So we should be careful about the Lukan theology of prayer. If she had prayed only, nothing could have happened. Luke tames "this story of an unconventional woman and casts her in a docile and acceptable role as an example of praying always, much like Anna, who spent eighty-four years praying in the Temple (Lk 2:36-38). Although Luke preserves the most stories with female characters, for the most part, they are given silent, passive roles.[7] Rather, she is "a powerful portrait of a godly widow persistently pursuing justice."[8]

As seen before, this parable proper was used by Luke and emphasizes the importance of prayer and not to lose heart (18:1).

---

7. Barbara Reid, *Parables for Preachers*, Year C, 234-5.

8. Ibid., 235.

It may be related to the importance of her prayer if prayer involves both words and actions. The main force of the parable proper is not the usual sense of prayer to God. Rather, she seeks justice persistently. This widow is atypical because widows are expected to receive supplies if any in their passive waiting; she does not wait for justice in her seat and pray to God in her cell. Rather, she confronts evil by visiting the judge. But Luke does not pick up that much of her radical action for justice. Instead, she becomes a model of prayer to the Lukan community and theology.

Questions for Reflection/Discussion

1. What would be the best title of this parable?
2. Why is justice important to her?
3. What can you say about Lukan interpretation of the parable proper with a focus on the importance of prayer?
4. Can you read this parable with the Canaanite woman's story in Matthew 15:21-28?

Pharisee and Tax-Collector

Luke 18:9-14

9 He also told this parable to some who trusted in themselves that they were righteous and regarded others with contempt: 10 "Two men went up to the temple to pray, one a Pharisee and the other a tax collector. 11 The Pharisee, standing by himself, was praying thus, 'God, I thank you that I am not like other people: thieves, rogues, adulterers, or even like this tax collector. 12 I fast twice a week; I give a tenth of all my income.' 13 But the tax collector, standing far off, would not even look up to heaven, but was beating his breast and saying, 'God, be merciful to me, a sinner!' 14 I tell you, this man went down to his home justified rather than the other; *for all*

LUKAN UNIQUE PARABLES (II)

who exalt themselves will be humbled, but all who humble themselves will be exalted." (Italics indicate the Lukan addition to the parable proper).

The original parable includes only 18:10-14a, and the rest (v.9, 14b) may be a Lukan creation. The theme of righteousness brackets v.9 and 14a, and therefore it may be the case the original is framed with that (*inclusio*). Verse 14b is a free-floating proverb (as in Matt 23:12; also Luke 14:11).

Tax Collectors are dubbed immoral people in Jewish society because they collect too much tax for Rome and do not care about the everyday people's lives. The Pharisees are the most religious people who seek the renewal of Judaism based on the Law.[9] Both the Pharisee and the Tax Collector enter the Temple to pray—a place of restoration and worship. But their prayers are different. The Pharisee's prayer looks like an excellent prayer. He regularly fasts and gives a tithing.[10] His prayer is compared to that of the Talmud: "I give thanks to thee, O Lord my God, that thou hast given me my lot with those who sit in the seat of learning, and not with those who sit at the street corners; for I am early to work, and they are early to work; I am early to work on words of the Torah and they are early to work on things of no moment."[11] Similarly, R. Judah says: "A man must recite three benedictions every day: 'Blessed be You, Lord, who did not make me a gentile. Blessed be You, Lord, who did not make me uneducated. Blessed be You,

---

9. In Luke, the Pharisees are both positive and negative. Jesus is invited by the Pharisee for dinner and talks with him. At most other times, however, the Pharisees appear confronting Jesus. Historically speaking, they are reformers of Judaism with a focus on the strict observance of the law, especially concerning Sabbath observance, dietary regulations, ritual purity, and the right interpretation of the Torah.

10. Fasting in Jewish tradition is done on various occasions: as a means of access to God (Lev 16:29; 23:27); supplication (Ps 35:13); expression of penance (2 Sam 12:13-25; 1 Kgs 21:27); mourning at the death of Saul (2 Sam 1:12). According to *Didache* 8:1, early Christians fasted twice a week, Wednesday and Friday. Tithing is also an important religious duty (Deut 14:22-23).

11. Talmud, b. Ber 28b. Similarly in Qumran Thanksgiving Hymns, 1QH 7:34; 15:34.

Lord, who did not make me a woman.'"[12] The Pharisee feels great and blessed because he lives by his faith. He is not a hypocrite.

But from the perspective of the marginalized, his prayer sounds too self-centered to see others with the eyes of mercy. He repeats the first pronoun "I" in his prayer": "God, I thank you that I am not like other people: thieves, rogues, adulterers, or even like this tax collector. I fast twice a week; I give a tenth of all my income" (Lk 18:11-12). It is not wrong that the Pharisee thanks God for his life and identity. But the issue is that his thankful prayer involves no sense of pity or empathy to those who are unlike him: "thieves, rogues, adulterers, or even like this tax collector." He could pray like this: "Lord, forgive them and give them your mercy so they may change their lives to turn to you; they don't know what they do." So here the question is: Is the Pharisee justified by God with this prayer and attitude toward others? His problem is not to see the God of mercy and compassion toward the marginalized. He must feel he is also small in front of God and others. He should know that he is a weak human being who needs the mercy of God every day. In this sense, he does not stand right before God because he is self-focused without looking at the poor status of his being and the need of mercy for others. The Pharisee does not see the marginalized (thieves, rogues, adulterers, tax collectors) as among people of God. They are simply viewed as the "dangerous" objects that must be avoided in society.[13]

The tax collector's prayer is terse with no elaboration or thanksgiving: "God, be merciful to me, a sinner!" (18:13). His prayer is a simple cry for mercy with the spirit of Ps 51: "Have

---

12. Tosefta, Ber. 6.18

13. For the Pharisees there must be a clear boundary between the sacred and the profane and between good people and bad people. But Jesus differs from the Pharisees' strict observance of the law and interprets it through the spirit of the law intended by God. For example, Jesus heals the sick on the Sabbath, and his justification for break the law and rationale for his healing is expressed like this in Mark: "The Sabbath was made for humans, and not humans for the Sabbath" (Mk 2:27). Jesus's point is that the law should be kept for humans, after a careful discernment that lifts the value of humanity. Otherwise, the law cannot be kept for the sake of the law.

mercy on me, God, in your goodness; in your abundant compassion blot out my offense." All he wants is God's mercy, confessing that he is a sinner! What else he needs when he stands before God? No matter who stands before God, what is needed is the mercy of God, because no one is perfect before God. But with this man the tax collector, the mercy of God is everything because he knows what he did wrong before God and other people. So he does not even look up to heaven because he feels he is no-one. So he beats his breast and cries to God for mercy. He knows now what he is: a sinner. He knows he is despised by the Pharisee and others because he is supposed to be greedy, sinful, unclean, and dishonest. But he also knows the only hope is to seek the mercy of God and to change the course of his life toward God. Because of this realization, he is declared to be right in his relationship with God. Yes, he was wrong in his former life, but now because he changes his mind, he is given the new opportunity to live as God's child. Otherwise, the declaration of this man's righteousness requires his moral life. His new life can begin now with that humbling realization he is no-one before God, seeking God's justice in the world.

In conclusion, Jesus makes this story happen in the temple which is the holy place of restoration and sanctification for Jewish people. The temple is not a place of separation or self-pride. It is the place that a person can meet the God of mercy with the heart of humility. The one who is righteous is not merely someone who keeps the law but someone whose heart is renewed through God's mercy and ready to live a new life because of it. A new life in God starts with a change of heart.

This parable of the Pharisee and Tax Collector echoes an important Lukan theology on the kingdom of God: God's compassion for all. Because of this theology, the goal of life is not to feel happiness by comparing with others. What is wrong with the Pharisee is not because he was a Pharisee keeping the laws so meticulously, but because he was not in solidarity with the sinner, the tax collector. He did not have the heart of mercy. From another note, he was just like a rich farmer in the earlier parable in Luke, who did not see the need of others. So the right attitude and prayer need humbleness before God and others. From the Lukan perspective, what is lacking with the Pharisee is the vision of God's rule for all.

Questions for Reflection/Discussion

1. What is the main problem of the Pharisee's prayer? What about his attitude toward the tax collector?
2. What is good prayer?
3. Why is the tax collector justified before God?

Bibliography

Batten, Alicia. "Dishonor, Gender and the Parable of the Prodigal Son." *Toronto Journal of Theology* 13.2 (1997) 187-200.
Borg, Marcus. *Jesus: The Life, Teaching, and Relevance of a Religious Revolutionary*. New York: HaperCollins, 2008.
Buttrick, David. *Speaking Parables: A Homiletic Guide*. Louisville, KY: WJKP, 2000.
Calvin, John. *Commentary on a Harmony of the Evangelists: Matthew, Mark, and Luke* Vol. 3. Edinburgh: Calvin Translation Society, 1846.
Carlston, Charles. "Reminiscence and Redaction in Luke 15:11-32." *JBL* 94 (1975) 368-90.
Carpenter, John. "The Parable of the Talents in Missionary Perspective: A Call for an Economic Spirituality," *Missiology* 25.2 (1997) 165-181.
Carson, D. A. "Matthew," in *The Expositor's Bible Commentary*, vol. 8. Grand Rapids: Zondervan, 1984.
Carter, Warren. *Matthew and the Margins: A Socio-Political and Religious Reading*. Sheffield: Sheffield Academic Press, 2000.
Chrysostom, John. *Homilies on Matthew* in *Nicene and Post-Nicene Fathers* Vol. 10. Grand Rapids: Eerdmans, 1978.
Cranfield, Charles. "The Good Samaritan," *Theology Today*, 11.3 (1954) 368-372.
Crossan, John Dominic. *In Parables: The Challenge of the Historical Jesus*. New York: Harper & Row, 1973.
Davies, W.D and Dale Allison, *A Critical and Exegetical Commentary on the Gospel According to Matthew*, Vol. 3 (London: T & T Clark, 1997), 402-403.
De Boer, Martinus. "Ten thousand talents: Matthew's interpretation and redaction of the parable of the Unforgiving Servant(Matt 18:23-35)." *CBQ* 50.2 (1988) 214-232.
Dodd, C.H. (Charles Harold). *The Parables of the Kingdom*. Rev. ed. 1936. London;: James Nisbet & Co.; Fontana, 1961.
Doty, William. "An Interpretation: Parable of the Weeds and Wheat." *Interpretation* 25.2 (1971) 185-193.

BIBLIOGRAPHY

Duff, Nancy. "Luke 15:11-32," *Interpretation* 49.1 (1995) 66-69;
Eliade, Mircea. *The Sacred and the Profane: The Nature of Religion*. Orlando, FL: Harcourt, 1987.
Findlay, Alexander. *Jesus and His Parables*. London: Epworth Press, 1950.
Fitzmyer, Joseph. *The Gospel According to Luke*. New York: Doubleday, 1985.
Foucault, Michael. *The Order of Things*. New York: Pantheon, 1970.
Fox, Eric. "The Parable of the Lost or Wandering Sheep: Matthew 18:10-14; Luke 15:3-7." *Anglican Theological Review* 44.1 (1962) 44-57.
Funk, Robert W. *The Parables of Jesus*. Polebridge Press, 1988.
_____. "Beyond Criticism in Quest of Literacy: the Parable of the Leaven," *Interpretation* 25.2 (1971) 149-170.
_____. "The Good Samaritan as Metaphor." *Semeia* 2 (1974): 74-81.
Funk, Robert W., Bernard Brandon Scott, and James R. Butts, eds. *The Parables of Jesus: Red Letter Edition: A Report of the Jesus Seminar*. Sonoma, Calif.: Polebridge Press, 198
González, Gusto. *Tres meses en la escuela de Mateo*. Nashville Abingdon Press, 1996.
Gowler, David B. *What Are They Saying About the Parables?* New York; Mahwah: Paulist Press, 2000.
Grant, Robert and D. Freedman, *The Secret Sayings of Jesus according to the Gospel of Thomas*. London, 1960.
Hanson, K.C. "Kinship." *BTB* 24 (1994) 183-94.
Harrington, Daniel. *The Gospel of Matthew*, Collegeville, MN: Liturgical Press, 1991
Heil, John. "Reader-Response and the Narrative Context of the Parables about Growing Seed in Mark 4:1-34," *Catholic Biblical Quarterly* 54.2 (1992) 271-286.
Herzog, William R. *Parables as Subversive Speech: Jesus as Pedagogue of the Oppressed*. Louisville: Westminster/John Knox Press, 1994.
_____. "Sowing Discord: The Parable of the Sower (Mark 4:1-9)," *Review and Expositor* 109.2 (2012) 187-198.
Hultgren, Arland J. *The Parables of Jesus: A Commentary*. Grand Rapids, MI: Eerdmans, 2000.
Hunter, A.M. (Archibald Macbride). *The Parables: Then and Now*. London: SCM Press, 1971.
Jeremias, Joachim. *The Parables of Jesus*. Translated by S.H. Hooke. New York, NY: Charles Scribner's Sons, 1955.
_____. *Jerusalem in the Time of Jesus. An Investigation into Social and Economic Conditions during the New Testament Period*. Philadelphia: Fortress, 1969.
_____. "Tradition und Redaktion in Lukas 15." *Zeitschrift für die neutesamentliche Wissenschaft* 62 (1971) 172-89.
_____. "Zum Gleichnis vom verlorenen Sohn, Luk. 15, 11-32," *Theologische Zeitschrift* 5 (1949) 228-31.
Jerome. *The Letters of St. Jerome*, vol. 1, edited by Johannes Quasten and Walter J. Burghardt. Mahwah, NJ: Paulist Press, 1963.

BIBLIOGRAPHY

Jiménez, Pablo. "The Laborers of the Vineyard (Matthew 20:1-16): A Hispanic Homiletical Reading," *Journal for Preachers* 21.1 (1997) 35-40.

Johnson, Luke Timothy. *The Gospel of Luke* (Collegeville, MN: Liturgical Press, 1991)

Jones, J.R. "Love as Perception of Meaning," *Religion and Understanding*. New York, NY: MacMillan, 1967.

Juel, Donald. "The Strange Silence of the Bible." *Interpretation* 51.1 (1997) 5-19.

Jülicher, Adolf. *Die Gleichnisreden Jesu*. 2. Aufl. 1963. Tübingen: Mohr Siebeck, 1910.

Kim, Yung Suk. *Biblical Interpretation: Theory, Process, and Criteria*. Eugene, OR: Pickwick, 2013.

_____. *Christ's Body in Corinth: The Politics of a Metaphor*. Minneapolis, MN: Fortress, 2008.

_____. *Truth, Testimony, and Transformation: A New Reading of the "I Am" Sayings of Jesus in the Fourth Gospel*. Eugene, OR: Cascade, 2014.

Kloppenborg, John S. *Q the Earliest Gospel* (Louisville and London: W/JKP, 2008)

Knight, George. "Luke 16:19-31: The Rich Man and Lazarus." *Review and Expositor* 94.2 (1997) 277-283.

LaHurd, Carol."Re-viewing Luke 15 with Arab Christian Women." In *A Feminist Companion to Luke*, edited by Amy-Jill Levine, 246-268. New York: Sheffield Academic, 2002.

Landry, David, and Ben May. "Honor Restored: New Light on the Parable of the Prudent Steward (Luke 16:1-8a)." *JBL* 119.2 (2000) 287-309.

Levine, Amy-Jill. *Short Stories by Jesus: The Enigmatic Parables of a Controversial Rabbi*. New York, NY: HarperOne, 2014.

Loader, William. "First Thoughts on Passages from Matthew in the Lectionary," http://wwwstaff.murdoch.edu.au/~loader/MtPent14.htm. Accessed on May 8, 2015.

Malina, Bruce and John Pilch. *Social-Science Commentary on the Synoptic Gospels*. Minneapolis, MN: Fortress Press, 1992.

McArthur, Harvey K. "The Parable of the Mustard Seed." *CBQ* 33 (1971) 198-201.

McGaughy, Lane C. "The Fear of Yahweh and the Mission of Judaism: A Postexilic Maxim and Its Early Christian Expansion in the Parable of the Talents," *JBL* 94.2 (1975) 235-245.

McIver, Robert K. "The parable of the weeds among the wheat (Matt 13:24-30, 36-43) and the relationship between the kingdom and the church as portrayed in the Gospel of Matthew." *JBL* 114.4 (1995) 643-659.

Meier, John. "The Parable of the Wheat and the Weeds (Matthew 13:24-30): Is Thomas's Version (Logion 57) Independent?" *JBL* 131.4 (2012) 715-732.

Metzger, Bruce. *A Textual Commentary on the Greek New Testament*. New York, NY: Hendrickson, 2005.

BIBLIOGRAPHY

Neyrey, Jerome. "First-Century Personality." In *The Social World of Luke-Acts: Models for Interpretation,* edited by Jerome Neyrey, 67-96. Peabody, MA: Hendrickson Publishers, 1999.

Oesterley, W.O.E. *The Gospel Parables in the Light of their Jewish Background.* New York, NY: Macmillian, 1936.

O'Rourke, John. "Some Notes on Luke 15:11-32." *NTS* 18.4 (1972) 431-433.

Park, Rohun. "Revisiting the parable of the prodigal son for decolonization: Luke's reconfiguration of *oikos* in Luke 15:11-32," *Biblical Interpretation* 17 (2009) 507-520.

Parsons, Mikeal. "The Prodigal's Older Brother: The History and Ethics of Reading Luke 15:25- 32." *Perspectives in Religious Studies* 23 (1996) 147-174.

Payne, Philip. "Order of Sowing and Ploughing in the Parable of the Sower." *NTS* 25.1 (1978) 123-29.

Perrin, Norman. *Rediscovering the Teaching of Jesus.* New York: Harper & Row, 1967.

Peterson, William L. "The Parable of the Lost Sheep in the Gospel of Thomas and the Synoptics." *Novum Testamentum* 23.2 (1981) 128-47.

Powelson, Mark and Ray Riegert eds. *The Lost Gospel Q: The Original Sayings of Jesus.* Berkeley, CA: Seastone, 1996.

Reid, Barbara. *Parables for Preachers,* Year A. Matthew. Collegeville, MN: Liturgical, 2001.

_____. Year B. Mark. 1999.

_____. Year C. Luke. 2000.

Räisänen, Heikki. "The Prodigal Gentile and His Jewish Christian Brother, Luke 15:11-32." In *The Four Gospels,* edited by F. Van Segbroek *et al.*, 1617-36. Leuven: Leuven University Press, 1992.

Matthew S. Rindge, "Luke's Artistic Parables: Narratives of Subversion, Imagination, and Transformation," *Interpretation* 68 (2014) 403-415.

Rodríguez, José. "The Parable of the Affirmative-Action Employer." *Apuntes* 8.3 (1988) 51-59.

Rohrbaugh, Richard L. "A Peasant Reading of the Parable of the Talents/Pounds: A Text of Terror?" *BTB* 23.1 (1993) 32-39.

Sanders, Jack T. "Tradition and Redaction in Luke 15:11-32." *NTS* 15 (1968-69) 433-38.

_____. "The Parable of the Pounds and Lukan Anti-Semitism." *TS* 42 (1981): 660-68.

Schellenberg, Ryan. "Kingdom as Contaminant? The Role of Repertoire in the Parables of the Mustard Seed and the Leaven." *CBQ* 71.3 (2009) 527-543.

Schottroff, Luise. "Das Gleichnis vom verlorenen Sohn." *Zeitschrift für Theologie und Kirche* 68 (1971) 27-52.

_____. *The Parables of Jesus.* Minneapolis: Fortress, 2006.

Schweitzer, Albert. *The Quest of the Historical Jesus.* New York: Macmillan, 1968.

Bibliography

Schweizer, Eduardo. *The Good News According to Matthew*. Louisville, KY: WJKP, 1975.

Scott, Bernard. "Lost Junk, Found Treasure," *TBT* 26 (1988) 31-34.

———. "The King's accounting: Matthew 18:23-34." *JBL* 104.3 (1985) 429-442.

———. *Hear Then the Parable: A Commentary on the Parables of Jesus*. Minneapolis: Fortress Press, 1989.

———. *Re-Imagine the World: An Introduction to the Parables of Jesus*. Santa Rosa, Calif.: Polebridge Press, 2001.

Snodgrass, Klyne R. *Stories with Intent: A Comprehensive Guide to the Parables of Jesus*. Grand Rapids, MI: Eerdmans, 2008.

Spicq, C. *Dieu et l'homme selon le Nouveau Testament* (Paris: Cerf, 1960)

Tannehill, Robert. *Luke*. Nashville, TN: Abingdon Press, 1996.

Tevel, J. M. "The Laborers in the Vineyard: the Exegesis of Matthew 20:1-7 in the Early Church," *Vigiliae Christianae* 46 (1992) 356-380.

Ukpong, Justin. "The Parable of the Talents (Matt 25:14-30): Commendation or Critique of Exploitation?: A Social-Historical and Theological Reading." *Neotestamenica* 46.1 (2012) 190-207.

Waller, Elizabeth. "The parable of the leaven: a sectarian teaching and the inclusion of women," *Union Seminary Quarterly Review* 35.1-2 (1979-80) 99-109.

Weder, Hans. *Die Gleichnisse Jesu als Metaphern: Traditions-und redaktionsgeschichtliche Analysen und Interpretationen*. Göttingen: Vandenhoeck & Ruprecht, 1978.

Westermann, Claus. The Parables of Jesus in the Light of the Old Testament. Minneapolis, MN: Fortress, 1990.

Wilder, Amos. *Early Christian Rhetoric: The Language of the Gospel*. Eugene, OR: Wipf & Stock, 2014.

———. "The Parable of the Sower: Naïveté and Method in Interpretation." *Semeia* 2 (1974) 134-51.

Young, Brad. *The Parables: Jewish Tradition and Christian Interpretation*. Peabody, MA: Hendrickson Publishers, 1998.

www.ingramcontent.com/pod-product-compliance
Lightning Source LLC
Chambersburg PA
CBHW070501090426
42735CB00012B/2643